GnuCash 2.6 Tutorial and Concepts Guide

A catalogue record for this book is available from the Hong Kong Public Libraries.
Published in Hong Kong by Samurai Media Limited.
Email: info@samuraimedia.org

ISBN 978-988-8381-92-0

Table of Contents

List of Figures

List of Tables

Part I. Getting Started

Table of Contents

Chapter 1. Overview

Introduction

GnuCash is the personal finance software package made for you. It is versatile enough to keep track of all your financial information, from the simple to the very complex. It is one of the few financial software packages that supports global currencies, and it is the only open-source program of its kind. Best of all, GnuCash is easy to learn and use!

So, what can GnuCash do for you? It can keep track of your personal finances in as much detail as you prefer. If you are just starting out, use GnuCash to keep track of your checkbook. You may then decide to track cash as well as credit card purchases to better determine where your money is being spent. When you start investing, you can use GnuCash to help monitor your portfolio. Buying a vehicle or a home? GnuCash will help you plan the investment and track loan payments. If your financial records span the globe, GnuCash provides all the multiple-currency support you need.

This image shows a Chart of Accounts with multiple currencies and investments.

While GnuCash is well suited for personal finances, it is also powerful enough for business use. There are many business features, from integrated accounts receivable and payable systems, to tax table construction. You will find these and the many other business features surprisingly powerful and easy to use.

Features

Easy to Use

Within a matter of minutes you will be able to enter your personal finance information and generate color graphs that represent your financial status. If you can use the register in the back of your checkbook - you can use GnuCash! Type directly into the register, tab between fields, and use quick-fill to automatically complete transactions. The interface is customizable from within the application itself.

- *Easy to Use Menus*: GnuCash menus conform to the GNOME Human Interface Guidelines. This means that they are simple and similar in appearance to many other GNOME applications.

- *Documentation*: GnuCash has built-in Help and extensive User's Guide documentation.

- *Import Methods*: GnuCash supports many ways to input transactions besides manual entry. If you can access your bank accounts on-line, this is especially useful, as most banks and credit card companies support one of the following import methods. You will spend less time entering data and more time analyzing results.

  - *Quicken Import File (QIF)*: Import Quicken QIF style files, a popular file format with many commercial personal finance software packages.

  - *Open Financial Exchange (OFX)*: GnuCash is the first free software application to support the Open Financial Exchange protocol. Many financial institutions are moving towards this format.

  - *Home Banking Computer Interface (HBCI)*: GnuCash is the first free software application to support the German Home Banking Computer Interface protocol. This protocol includes statement download, initiates bank transfers, and makes direct debits possible.

- *Reports*: GnuCash comes with over 30 prebuilt reports, including Account Summary, Income, Expenses, Transaction Report, Balance Sheet, Profit&Loss, Portfolio Valuation, and many others. Reports support graphical views of the data, including pie charts, bar charts, and scatter plots. The reports can be exported to HTML files, and are easily customized.

- *Scheduled Transactions*: GnuCash now has the ability to automatically create and enter transactions, or remind you when these transactions are due, giving you the choice of entering, postponing or removing the automated transaction.

- *Mortgage and Loan Repayment Assistant*: Used to set up a variable payment loan scheduled transaction.

- *Easy Account Reconciliation*: Integrated reconciliation makes reconciling your GnuCash accounts with statements simple and effective.

- *Multi-platform Compatibility*: GnuCash is supported on a variety of platforms and operating systems. The list of fully supported operating systems (and platforms) for GnuCash 2.6.8 is: GNU/Linux (x86, x86_64, Sparc, PPC), FreeBSD (x86, x86_64), OpenBSD (x86, x86_64), Solaris (Sparc), and MacOS X (Intel, PPC). Previous versions of GnuCash have been known to work with, SGI IRIX (MIPS), IBM AIX 4.1.5 (RS/6000), Unixware 7 (Intel), and SCO OpenServer 5.0.4 (Intel), but their current status is unknown.

Tracks Your Investments

GnuCash includes a number of investment features that allow you to track all your investments. With GnuCash you can track stocks individually (one per account) or in a portfolio of accounts (a group of accounts that can be displayed together).

GnuCash supports online stock and mutual fund quotes. This means you no longer need to look up stock prices one at a time. The process can be automated, and you can see the latest value of your stocks.

International Support

GnuCash is truly an application that works with and understands users from all around the world. There are many built-in features to facilitate interaction with the international world we live in today.

- *Native Languages*: GnuCash has been fully translated into 12 languages: Chinese, Czech, Dutch, English, French, German, Italian, Portuguese, Russian, Slovak, Spanish and Swedish. More than 25 other languages are partially supported.

- *International Format Handling*: GnuCash understands that different countries display the date and numbers differently. You are able to work with the date and number formats you are accustomed to.

- *Multiple Currencies and Currency Trading*: Multiple currencies are supported and can be bought and sold (traded). Currency movements between accounts remain fully balanced if "Trading Accounts" is enabled.

- *On-line exchange rates*: With GnuCash, you no longer need look up your exchange rates one at a time. The process can be automated, to always present you with the account values converted to your preferred currency using the latest exchange rates.

Business Support

GnuCash has many features to support the needs of the business accounting community.

- *Accounts Receivable/Payable*: GnuCash has an integrated Accounts Receivable and Accounts Payable system. You can track Customers, Vendors, Invoicing and Bill Payment, and use different Tax and Billing Terms in a small business.

- *Depreciation*: GnuCash can track depreciation of capital assets.

- *Reports*: GnuCash offers a wide variety of ready-to-use business reports.

Accounting Features

For those knowledgeable in accounting, here is a list of GnuCash's accounting features.

- *Double Entry*: Every transaction must debit one account and credit others by an equal amount. This ensures the "books balance" - that the difference between income and expense exactly equals the sum of all bank, cash, stock and other assets.

- *Split Transactions*: A single transaction can be split into several pieces to record taxes, fees, and other compound entries.

- *Chart of Accounts*: A master account can have a hierarchy of detail accounts underneath it. This allows similar account types such as Cash, Bank, or Stock to be grouped into a master account such as "Assets".

- *General Ledger*: One register window can display multiple accounts at the same time. This eases the trouble of tracking down typing/entry errors. It also provides a convenient way of viewing a portfolio of many stocks, by showing all transactions in that portfolio.

- *Income/Expense Account Types (Categories)*: These categorize your cash flow and, when used properly with the double-entry feature, will provide an accurate Profit&Loss statement.

What's New in 2.6

- GnuCash is available on Windows.

- The GnuCash file format is incompatible with versions earlier than 2.1.2. Specifically, scheduled transactions are stored differently. Using version 2.6, you can upgrade your older GnuCash file to the new format.

- More translations.

- Improved report handling.

- Fixed lots of crashes.

- Improved multi-currency support.

- Enhanced QIF import.

See http://wiki.gnucash.org/wiki/Release_Schedule#Release_Schedule_for_2.2.x for detailed lists of improvements made in this series.

What's New in v2.0

- *Gnome 2.0 (Gtk2)*

GnuCash is now using the latest tool-kits from gtk, and follows the normal Gnome2 HIG standards.

- *UTF-8 support*

GnuCash now stores and reads each country's special character sets by using UTF-8.

- *Budget*

GnuCash now comes with a budget feature that can help you keep your expenses under control.

- *Import of MT940 files*

Data files with transactions in MT940 format (as can be downloaded from some banks) can now be imported into GnuCash.

- *Bug fixes*

GnuCash is now more stable and secure than ever before due to the long testing phase before we reached 2.0, as well as using more stable and mature libraries (gtk2 for instance). Numerous corrections has been made in every part of GnuCash, and too many for us to highlight any special area.

About this Book

This manual's goal is to save you time. It will get you started using GnuCash as quickly as possible.

Each chapter follows a simple format. A chapter begins with a "Concepts" discussion which introduces general themes and terminology, addressed and used within that chapter. "How-To" sections, which address specific procedures follow. Finally, a "Putting It All Together" section ends the chapter by giving detailed, concrete examples.

Beginning users will find the "Concepts" sections very helpful. They provide a reference for good ways to track your finances, and serve as a general introduction to financial background and terminology. Experienced users can flip to the "How-To" sections to quickly scan procedures. These sections provide to-the-point steps for accomplishing specific tasks. The "Putting It All Together" sections present real-world examples in the form of a tutorial. Beginning with creation of a file in Chapter 2, *The Basics*, each successive chapter builds on the previous chapter's tutorial.

This manual is organized into 3 main parts:

- *Getting Started*

- *Managing Personal Finances*

- *Managing Business Finances*.

Getting Started provides you with the most basic information needed to begin using GnuCash. The chapters in this section explain concepts that are fundamental to using GnuCash. New users of GnuCash should familiarize themselves with the information in these chapters to get you up and running:

- Chapter 1, *Overview* - (this chapter) gives a general overview of GnuCash

- Chapter 2, *The Basics* - gives users a very brief introduction to accounting principles, and then provides information about how GnuCash structures its data. There is also information on basic interface elements in GnuCash. Finally, this chapter explains how GnuCash stores and manages your data.

- Chapter 3, *Accounts* - gives further information about accounts and how to organize them.

- Chapter 4, *Transactions* - gives basic information about transactions and how to enter them.

Managing Personal Finances addresses common applications and features of GnuCash in greater detail. You will see more specific cases, based on frequently asked questions about applying GnuCash to everyday situations. Here are the applications and features covered in this part:

- Chapter 5, *Checkbook*

- Chapter 6, *Credit Cards*

- Chapter 7, *Loans*

- Chapter 8, *Investments*

- Chapter 9, *Capital Gains*

- Chapter 10, *Multiple Currencies*

Managing Business Finances discusses the use of GnuCash in business accounting:

- Chapter 11, *Business Introduction*

- Chapter 12, *Business Setup*

- Chapter 13, *Accounts Receivable*

- Chapter 14, *Accounts Payable*

- Chapter 15, *Payroll*

- Chapter 16, *Budgets*

- Chapter 17, *Other Assets*

- Chapter 18, *Depreciation*

- Chapter 19, *Python Bindings*

- Chapter 20, *Importing Business Data*

This manual also includes several appendices, which contains extra information you might want to know:

- Appendix A, *Migration Guide* - Guide for former Quicken®, MS Money or other QIF users

- Appendix B, *Frequently Asked Questions*

- Appendix C, *Contributed Account Trees*

- Appendix D, *Auxiliary File Formats*

- Appendix E, *GNU Free Documentation License*

Last, but not least, a glossary and index help you quickly locate topics.

Top Ten Reasons to Use GnuCash

We've already discussed some of the general advantages of using GnuCash. Here are some specific features offered by GnuCash that may not exist in other programs.

1. Simple user interface

    GnuCash is as easy to use as a checkbook register. It's simpler than a paper register, because auto-completion and other entry shortcuts not only do work for you, but reduce data entry errors.

2. Easy import

    GnuCash allows you to import data from on-line bank statements and software packages using QIF (Quicken® Interchange Format), OFX and HBCI files. An easy-to-use "assistant" walks you through reviewing resulting changes and actually importing them into GnuCash.

3. Statement reconciliation

    Reconcile monthly statements quickly by entering the statement ending balance and checking off transactions. GnuCash helps you catch any discrepancies between your data and statements you receive.

4. Investment tracking

    GnuCash offers a host of ways to track your investment portfolio. Special investment accounts simplify data entry, and on-line tools allow you to update prices of your holdings as the markets change. Reports complete the picture, allowing you to analyze your investment decisions.

5. Multiple currency support

    GnuCash allows you to track multiple currencies. If you have bank accounts, investments or other financial data in different currencies, use GnuCash to monitor them.

6. Customized reports and graphs

    Reports and graphs give you valuable information for filing taxes, budgeting, or simply figuring out where your money goes. GnuCash offers a variety of easy-to-use reports and graphs to help analyze your financial position. It gives you the freedom to customize your own reports to suit your unique needs.

7. Double entry

    To provide complete records, GnuCash uses the double entry method of bookkeeping. Double entry simply means that money doesn't just appear or disappear - an equal amount must come from one location and go to another location. By tracking the transaction in both locations, GnuCash will give you detailed reports from the perspective of either account.

8. Sources of help

A Tip of the Day screen gives helpful tips to new users about GnuCash features. Within the program, a searchable Help menu guides you to information or connects to the GnuCash web page for further assistance. GnuCash also has strong, helpful developer and user communities who provide help through mailing lists as well as through the IRC channel.

9. Shortcuts

GnuCash offers many shortcuts to help you enter data. Type the first few characters of a common entry and GnuCash will automatically fill in the rest! You can also use copy, paste and duplicate functions to save typing time. Keyboard shortcuts let you quickly choose a menu option or to enter numerical data. Many numeric entry fields can act as a calculator: enter "92.18+33.26" and watch GnuCash input the corresponding sum for you!

10.Open source

GnuCash doesn't hide its methods. If you wonder how GnuCash computed a number, you can find it out. In addition, you can set preferences that tell GnuCash how much information to display to you. There is no "secret code" used in GnuCash - it continues to be an open-source program.

These are only a few of the advantages you'll discover when you start using GnuCash to track your financial information. Now get ready to enjoy the benefits of GnuCash for yourself!

Installation

Installation of GnuCash is usually simple.

The *GnuCash download page* [http://www.gnucash.org/download.phtml] contains detailed instructions on how to install GnuCash for each operating system supported.

Chapter 2. The Basics

This chapter will introduce some of the basics of using GnuCash. It is recommended that you read through this chapter, before starting to do any real work with GnuCash. Next chapters will begin to show you hands on examples.

Accounting Concepts

GnuCash is easy enough to use that you do not need to have a complete understanding of accounting principles to find it useful. However, you will find that some basic accounting knowledge will prove to be invaluable as GnuCash was designed using these principles as a template. It is highly recommended that you understand this section of the guide before proceeding.

The 5 Basic Accounts

Basic accounting rules group all finance related things into 5 fundamental types of "accounts". That is, everything that accounting deals with can be placed into one of these 5 accounts:

Account types

Assets	Things you own
Liabilities	Things you owe
Equity	Overall net worth
Income	Increases the value of your accounts
Expenses	Decreases the value of your accounts

It is clear that it is possible to categorize your financial world into these 5 groups. For example, the cash in your bank account is an asset, your mortgage is a liability, your paycheck is income, and the cost of dinner last night is an expense.

The Accounting Equation

With the 5 basic accounts defined, what is the relationship between them? How does one type of account affect the others? Firstly, equity is defined by assets and liability. That is, your net worth is calculated by subtracting your liabilities from your assets:

Assets - Liabilities = Equity

Furthermore, you can increase your equity through income, and decrease equity through expenses. This makes sense of course, when you receive a paycheck you become "richer" and when you pay for dinner you become "poorer". This is expressed mathematically in what is known as the Accounting Equation:

Assets - Liabilities = Equity + (Income - Expenses)

This equation must always be balanced, a condition that can only be satisfied if you enter values to multiple accounts. For example: if you receive money in the form of income you must see an equal increase in your assets. As another example, you could have an increase in assets if you have a parallel increase in liabilities.

Figure 2.1. The basic accounts relationships

A graphical view of the relationship between the 5 basic accounts. Net worth (equity) increases through income and decreases through expenses. The arrows represent the movement of value.

Double Entry

The accounting equation is the very heart of a *double entry accounting system*. For every change in value of one account in the Accounting Equation, there must be a balancing change in another. This concept is known as the *Principle of Balance*, and is of fundamental importance for understanding GnuCash and other double entry accounting systems. When you work with GnuCash, you will always be concerned with at least 2 accounts, to keep the accounting equation balanced.

Balancing changes (or transfers of money) among accounts are done by debiting one account and simultaneously crediting another. Accounting *debits* and *credits* do not mean "decrease" and "increase". Debits and credits each increase certain types of accounts and decrease others. In asset and expense accounts, debits increase the balance and credits decrease the balance. In liability, equity and income accounts, credits increase the balance and debits decrease the balance.

In traditional double-entry accounting, the left column in the register is used for debits, while the right column is used for credits. Accountants record increases in asset and expense accounts on the debit (left) side, and they record increases in liability, revenue, and equity accounts on the credit (right) side. GnuCash follows this convention in the register.

Note

This accounting terminology can be confusing to new users, which is why GnuCash allows you to use the common terms Deposit and Withdrawal. If you prefer the formal accounting terms, you can change the account register column headings to use them in the General tab under Preferences (see the GnuCash Help Manual for more information on setting preferences).

Warning

Common use of the words *debit* and *credit* does not match how accountants use these words. In common use, *credit* generally has positive associations; in accounting, *credit* means *affecting the right column* of the ledger sheet of an account. This is associated with a *decrease* in asset and expense, but an *increase* of income, liability and equity accounts.

For more details see http://en.wikipedia.org/wiki/Debits_and_credits.

Data Entry Concepts

When entering data in GnuCash, you should be aware of the 3 levels of organization in which GnuCash divides your data: files, accounts and transactions. These levels are presented in their order of complexity, one file contains many accounts and one account contains many transactions. This division is fundamental to understanding how to use GnuCash.

Files

GnuCash stores information at the highest level in files. A file can be stored on your computer either as a single XML file (in all versions of GnuCash), or in a SQL database (in GnuCash version 2.4 and higher).

Note

SQL is pronounced "sequel", so in spoken and written language we would say "a SQL database".

With the XML file format, GnuCash stores your data in an XML data file, usually in compressed format (although this can be changed in the General tab of the GnuCash Preferences).

With SQL storage, GnuCash stores your data in a SQL database under the database application you select (SQLite3, MySQL or PostgreSQL).

You will need one main file or database for each set of accounts you are maintaining. To learn how to create and manage GnuCash files, see the section called "Storing your financial data".

Note

If you think you might need more than one set of accounts, you might want to consult a professional accountant or bookkeeper before proceeding. Most users will probably have only one data file.

Backup files and log files are automatically generated by GnuCash when appropriate. Backup and log files are described in the section called "Backing Up and Recovering Data".

Accounts

An *account* keeps track of what you own, owe, spend or receive. Each GnuCash file can contain any number of accounts, and each account can contain many sub-accounts up to an arbitrary number of levels. This simple feature gives GnuCash much of its power in managing your finances, as you will see in later chapters.

Examples of accounts include: checking accounts, savings accounts, credit card accounts, mortgages, and loans. Each GnuCash account tracks the activity for that "real" account, and can inform you of its status.

In addition, accounts are also used to categorize the money you receive or spend. For example, you can create expense accounts to track the money you pay on utilities or groceries. Even though these are not accounts that receive statements, they allow you to determine how much money is being spent in each of these areas.

Accounts will be covered in more detail in Chapter 3, *Accounts*.

Transactions

A *transaction* represents the movement of money among accounts. Whenever you spend or receive money, or transfer money between accounts, that is a transaction.

Examples of transactions are: paying a phone bill, transferring money from savings to checking, buying a pizza, withdrawing money, and depositing a paycheck. Chapter 4, *Transactions* goes more in depth on how to enter transactions.

In double entry accounting, transactions always involve at least two accounts–a source account and a destination account. GnuCash manages this by inserting a line into the transaction for every account that is affected, and recording the amounts involved in each line. A line within a transaction that records the account and amount of money involved is called a *split*. A transaction can contain an arbitrary number of splits.

Note

Splits in transactions will be covered in the section called "Split Transaction Example"

Interface

The very first time you open GnuCash, you will see the Welcome to GnuCash! screen. From there, GnuCash provides other tools to help you easily find what you are looking for. Let's take a look at some of the common screens and screen boxes you will see.

Tip of the Day

GnuCash provides a Tip of the Day screen to give helpful hints for using the program:

This image shows the Tip of the Day.

These tips provide useful information for beginning users. To view more of the tips, click Forward to continue. If you do not wish to see this screen box on start-up, deselect the box next to Show tips at startup. When you have finished viewing the helpful tips, click Close to close the Tip of the Day screen.

Account Tree Window

You should now see the Accounts window, which appears as shown below. The exact layout of the account tree will depend on which default accounts you selected during the New Account Hierarchy Setup. In this example, the Common Accounts are shown.

This image shows the Accounts window.

The Account Tree window (also known as a Chart of Accounts, or CoA) provides an overview of the data contained in the current file. It contains a list of account names and their current balances.

From this window, you can open the register of any account either by double-clicking the account name, right clicking the account name and selecting Open Account from the menu, or by using the Open button on the toolbar. GnuCash allows you to have as many account registers open as you wish. For more information on using account registers, see the section called "Account Register Window".

Tip

Clicking the small triangle to the left of an account that has children will expand the tree view showing child accounts.

At the top of this window is the *Titlebar*, which displays the file name for this set of accounts (once you have saved the file.) Below that is the *Menubar*. You can access the menu options by either clicking on these menu headings or by using shortcuts and access keys (see the section called "Menu Shortcuts"). Next is the *Toolbar*, which contains buttons for the most common functions.

The account tree appears below the *Toolbar*. Once you have started creating accounts, the account names will appear in the account tree. You can customize which headings show up by using the small down-arrow at the far right just above the account tree.

At the bottom is the *Statusbar*, which tells you information about what you own (Net Assets) and how much money you have made (Profits).

Account Register Window

Account Register windows are used to enter and edit your account data. As the name suggests, they look similar to a checkbook register.

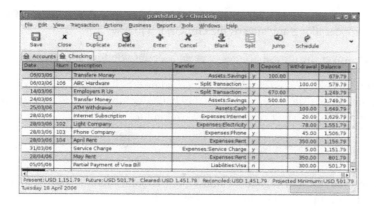

This image shows the Checking Account - Register with several transactions.

Chapter 4, *Transactions* explains more about account register windows and how to enter data into them. For now, note that the parts of an account register window are similar to the parts of the account tree window described earlier. The *Titlebar* at the top contains the account name. Below that, the *Menubar* contains menu options related to the account register. *Toolbar* buttons simplify common data entry functions. The *Statusbar* at the bottom of the window, displays some account balances covered in Chapter 4, *Transactions*. At the bottom of the account register window, information appears about the current location of the cursor.

Note

In the register windows, you can resize the various columns that GnuCash displays, but keep in mind that the description column will automatically expand to fill all unused space. Therefore you should increase the size of all your other columns first and then decrease the size of the description column.

Toolbar Buttons

Both the account tree window and the account register window contain *Toolbar* buttons. These buttons provide quick access to common functions such as Save and Open in the account tree window and Record and Delete in the account register window. If you are not sure what a button does, move the mouse pointer over that button, and you should see a description of the function appear.

Here is a summary of the account tree window buttons:

Account tree window buttons

Save	Save the current file to disk
Close	Close the current notebook page
Open, Edit, New and Delete	These are functions related to accounts. They are discussed in Chapter 3, *Accounts*.

Register-specific buttons are discussed in Chapter 4, *Transactions*.

Tab Bar

GnuCash uses a tabbed model that allows you to open multiple account registers and reports simultaneously. Each open window (which can include account registers, reports, or Scheduled

Transactions windows) is given a tab on this bar that you can click to view that window. Tabs can be configured in Preferences to appear along any side of the GnuCash window.

To see the full name for a tab, hover the mouse pointer over an account window tab.

If more screens are open than can be displayed across the screen, some tabs will not display. You can move through all tabs by clicking the arrows on either end of the tab bar. A complete list of tabs can be viewed by right-clicking the Tab Bar and any tab can be selected by clicking it.

Menu Items

The account tree window and the account register window both contain menu headings in a *Menubar*. Clicking on a menu heading brings up the menu items for that heading.

You can click on the account tree menu headings and then move the mouse pointer over the menu items to see what they do. As the pointer moves over a menu item, a description of the item appears in the lower left-hand corner of the window (inside the *Statusbar*). To select a menu item, click on it.

You can also access the most common menu items in a window by right-clicking the mouse anywhere in that window. In the account tree window, this will bring up a list of account items. In the account register window, this will bring up a list of transaction items.

Other ways of accessing menu items are through keyboard shortcuts and access keys, described next.

Menu Shortcuts

All of the menu items have access keys which are marked by underlined characters in the menu names. Pressing the **Alt** key with the underlined character in the menu heading will bring up the menu items for that heading. Once the menu items are displayed, type the underlined character in the menu item to activate it. For example, typing **Alt+F** in the main window brings up the File menu, then typing **S** will save the file. Access keys are fixed and cannot be changed by users.

Some of the more commonly used menu items also have shortcut keys that directly activate the command without having to traverse the menu structure. These shortcuts typically use the **Ctrl** key, although they can use any key combination. Menu shortcuts are displayed at the end of each menu item.

Getting Help

GnuCash offers help in many ways. We have already covered the Tip of the Day screen that gives you helpful hints upon start-up of your GnuCash session. GnuCash also offers an extensive help manual.

Help Manual

Once you have opened GnuCash, you will see the Account Tree window Help menu heading, which opens the Help manual. The Help manual is organized by topic, and you can expand each topic into its subtopics.

Topics are listed on the left side. To select a topic or subtopic, click on it, and you should see the text for that topic appear on the right. Use the Back and Forward buttons to navigate through your topic choices, and print any text using the Print button.

Web Access

The GnuCash Help window also acts as a simple web browser, so you can pull up a web site for additional information. You can open any web site under this window by clicking the Open *Toolbar* button and then typing in the URL. Use the Back, Forward, Reload, Stop, and Print buttons as you would in a standard browser.

The *GnuCash* [http://www.gnucash.org] web site contains helpful information about the program and about any updates to it. It also contains links to the GnuCash mailing lists for developers and users, and you can search the *archives of GnuCash mailing lists* [https://lists.gnucash.org/cgi-bin/namazu.cgi] for discussions on a particular topic. If you don't find the answers you are looking for, you can post your question to the *GnuCash user list* [https://lists.gnucash.org/mailman/listinfo/gnucash-user], and someone on the list will attempt to answer you.

The most updated GnuCash FAQ is also located on the *GnuCash FAQ website* [http://wiki.gnucash.org/wiki/FAQ], and contains answers to the popular questions.

Topic Search

The online manual also provides a search function. To search for a particular topic, click the Search tab at the bottom of the help window and type in your topic in the field provided. Click the Search button to complete your search. A list of choices should appear in the box below, clicking a choice will bring up its text on the right.

Storing your financial data

GnuCash is able to store your financial data in files or SQL databases so that they can be opened and modified at a later time. But first you need to create a container for your data.

Creating a file

To create a new GnuCash file do the following:

1. From the GnuCash *Menubar*, choose File → New File. The New Account Hierarchy setup assistant will start.

   ### Note

   If you are running GnuCash for the first time, you will be presented with the Welcome to GnuCash! screen. This screen is described in detail in the GnuCash manual.

2. Set your preferences in the assistant and move through the screens with the Forward, Cancel and Previous buttons.

Saving data

Follow these steps to save the file under your preferred name:

1. Choose File → Save As... from the *Menubar* or select the Save *Toolbar* button. GnuCash will bring up the save window.

2. Select the Data Format of the file you are saving from the drop down list. The default selection is XML but if you have set up a database back end you can change to that format.

   Depending on the selected Data Format the window can change as described in the following.

3.
   - If you selected XML or sqlite3 you will see a screen like this:

Figure 2.2. Save screen when XML or sqlite3 is selected.

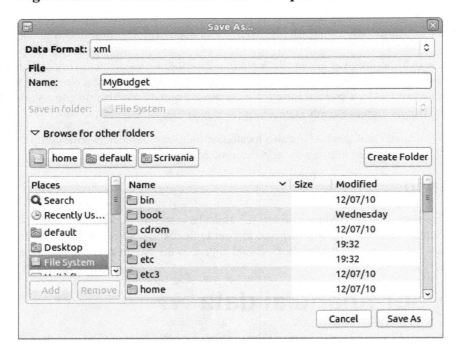

This image shows the Save screen when the selected Data Format is XML or sqlite3.

Type your chosen filename in the Name field. It is not necessary to specify an extension when you write the file name. GnuCash will automatically add the extension .gnucash to the file.

Note

The .gnucash extension was introduced in the 2.3 series of GnuCash. For already existing files, the extension will never be changed. So if you open an existing file named Myoldfile, that name won't be changed if the file is saved. You might use the Save As... command and give the file a new name in order to have it saved with the extension .gnucash.

Select the path where the file will be saved by browsing the tree in the lower panes.

Tip

Click on the Create Folder button to create a new folder with a custom name in the selected path.

- If you selected mysql or postgres Data Format you will see a screen like this:

Figure 2.3. Save screen when mysql or postgres is selected.

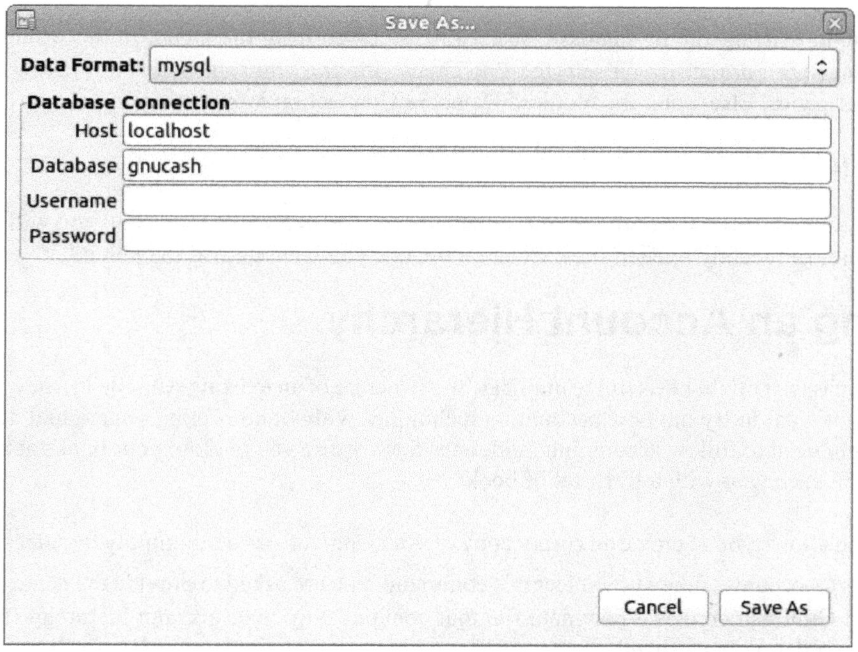

This image shows the Save screen when the selected Data Format is mysql or postgres.

Enter in this window the Database Connection information: Host, Database, Username and Password.

Warning

Saving to mysql or postgres requires the proper permissions in that database, that is you need to have the permissions to create a new database with the given database name, or you need to have write access to an existing database with the given database name.

4. Click the Save As button to save the file.

If you are keeping track of finances for a single household, you need only one file. But if you are also tracking business finances or want to keep data separate for some reason, then you will need more than one file.

Before ending each GnuCash session, be sure to save your data changes using File → Save or the Save *Toolbar* button.

Note

As it is very important to save your data frequently to avoid losing them for whatever reason, GnuCash is able to automatically save the opened file every a certain amount of time. This interval can be set in the General tab under Edit → Preferences (GnuCash → Preferences on Mac OS X). Keep in mind that this option is relevant only if you are saving in XML format. If you are working with a database, the Save button and the Save menu entry will be grayed out because changes are stored right away.

Opening data

To open an existing file or database, select File → Open from the menu. In the window that will open, select the Data Format. If you selected File choose the file you want to open by browsing the folders in the lower panes. Else, enter the required Database Connection information.

Tip

GnuCash keeps a list of the recently opened files. Open the File menu and you will see listed the names of recently opened files. Click on the one you want to load to open it.

Duplicating an Account Hierarchy

In some cases, it might be useful to duplicate the structure of an existing data file in a new file. For example, you might want to try out new accounting techniques without corrupting your actual accounting data, or you might need to follow accounting guidelines that require you to close your books at the end of the year and begin each year with a fresh set of books.

GnuCash allows you to create an empty copy of your Chart of Accounts simply by selecting File → Export → Export Accounts. When you select this command, you are asked to provide the name for the new empty file, and GnuCash creates a new data file that contains only your account hierarchy (that is, there is no transaction data). Once saved, the new file can be opened like any other GnuCash data file as described above.

Backing Up and Recovering Data

GnuCash creates several types of files to help ensure that your data is not lost. If you look in the folder where your saved file resides, you may see other files generated by GnuCash with the following extensions: .gnucash, .log, .LCK, .LNK in the same directory as your primary data file. What each of these files does is presented below.

Note

The following sections are relevant only if you are saving your financial data in the XML format

```
$ ls
myfile.gnucash
myfile.gnucash.20100414185747.gnucash
myfile.gnucash.20100414223248.log
myfile.gnucash.20100415114340.gnucash
myfile.gnucash.20100415154508.log
myfile.gnucash.20100415173322.gnucash
myfile.gnucash.20100415194251.log
myfile.gnucash.7f0982.12093.LNK
myfile.gnucash.LCK
```

Backup file (.gnucash)

Each time you save your data file, a backup copy will also be saved with the extension .YYYYMMDDHHMMSS.gnucash. This backup file is a complete copy of your previous data file, and the filename format refers to the data file, year, month, day and time of the backup. For example, the filename `myfile.gnucash.20100414185747.gnucash` indicates this is a backup copy of the file `myfile` saved in the year 2010, April 14, at 6:57:47 p.m.

To restore an old backup file, simply open the `.YYYYMMDDHHMMSS.gnucash` file with the date to which you wish to return. Be sure to save this file under a different name.

Note

`.YYYYMMDDHHMMSS.xac` instead of the actual extension `.YYYYMMDDHHMMSS.gnucash`. So if you upgrade from the 2.2 series to the 2.4 series, you may end up with both `.YYYYMMDDHHMMSS.xac` and `.YYYYMMDDHHMMSS.gnucash` backup files in your directory.

Log file (.log)

Each time you open and edit a file in GnuCash, GnuCash creates a log file of changes you have made to your data file. The log file uses a similar naming format as the backup files: `.YYYYMMDDHHMMSS.log`. Log files are not a full backup of your data file - they simply record changes you have made to the data file in the current GnuCash session.

In case you exit GnuCash inadvertently, possibly due to a power outage or a system wide crash, it is possible to recover most of your work since the last time you saved your GnuCash file using this log file. This is the procedure:

1. Open the last saved GnuCash file.

2. Go to File → Import → Replay GnuCash .log file and select the one .log file with the same date as the saved file you just opened. Make sure that you picked the right .log file, or you will possibly wreak havoc in your accounts.

Log replaying will recover any transaction affecting the balance entered since the last save, including those created from scheduled transactions and business features (invoices, bills, etc.).

Warning

Changes to the scheduled transactions, invoices or bills themselves are NOT recovered, and their transactions that were recovered may not be properly associated with them, and should thus be double-checked. Especially for business transactions, you may have to delete and re-create some of them. If you do not, although the balance will be correct, some reports may not.

Lock files (.LNK and .LCK)

You may occasionally see `.LNK` and `.LCK` files appear. These do not store any data, but they are created to prevent more than one user from opening the same file at the same time. These files are automatically created when you open the file, to lock it so no one else can access it. When you close your GnuCash session or open another file, GnuCash unlocks the first data file by deleting the `.LCK` and `.LNK` files.

If GnuCash crashes while you have a data file open, the `.LCK` and `.LNK` files are not deleted. The next time you try to open GnuCash, you will get a warning message that the file is locked. The warning message appears because the `.LNK` and `.LCK` files are still in your directory. It is safe to choose Yes to open the file, but you should delete the `.LNK` and `.LCK` files (using a terminal window or your file manager). Once those files are deleted, you will not get the warning message again unless GnuCash crashes.

File Management

So which files should you keep around? Keep your main data file, of course. It's a good idea to keep some of the more recent .YYYYMMDDHHMMSS.gnucash backup files, but you can safely delete the .log files since they are not complete copies of your data.

Note

If you upgraded from a GnuCash version prior to 2.4, you may also have backup files in the old .xac format. For these files you can apply the same principle described above for .YYYYMMDDHHMMSS.gnucash backup files.

You should also delete any .LCK and .LNK files that you see after closing GnuCash. If you decide to back up your data file to another disk manually, it's enough to back up the main data file - not the .YYYYMMDDHHMMSS.gnucash backup files.

Note

By default GnuCash will automatically delete any .log and .YYYYMMDDHHMMSS.gnucash backup files that are older than 30 days. You can change this behavior in the GnuCash preferences in the General tab under Edit → Preferences (GnuCash → Preferences on Mac OS X).

Migrating GnuCash data

Sometimes you may need to move your financial data and GnuCash settings to another machine. Typical use cases are when you buy a new computer or if you want to use the same settings over two different operating systems in a dual boot configuration.

Migrating financial data

Migrating GnuCash financial data is a as simple as copying .gnucash files with a file manager if you know where they are saved. If you can't remember where a file is stored but you can open it directly within GnuCash, save it in the desired path from within GnuCash.

All other files in the folder are either backups or log files. It won't do any harm to copy them too, but it's not likely to do any good, either.

Migrating preferences data

Preferences are stored in three different locations: one for GnuCash preferences, one for reports, and one for online banking settings. Preferences are managed by gsettings, reports are managed by GnuCash itself, and online banking is managed by aqbanking. If you do not use online banking, then you will not have this folder on your machine.

Where the GnuCash preferences are stored varies depending on your operating system (see Table 2.1, "Application Settings Locations", Table 2.2, "Saved Reports Locations", and Table 2.3, "Online Banking Settings Locations"). To back up and transfer your entire installation, you must copy these preferences as well.

Table 2.1. Application Settings Locations

Operating system	folder
Unix	GnuCash preferences are stored in dconf. You can use the commands dconf dump /org/

Operating system	folder
	gnucash/ on the old machine and dconf load /org/gnucash/ on the new machine to migrate your preferences.
Mac OSX	~/Library/Preferences/ gnucash.plist
Windows	The preferences are stored in the Windows registryHKEY_CURRENT_USER/software/ GSettings

Table 2.2. Saved Reports Locations

Operating system	folder
Unix	~/.gnucash
Mac OSX	~/Library/Application Support/ gnucash
Windows	Documents and Settings/ Username/.gnucash or Users/ Username/.gnucash

Table 2.3. Online Banking Settings Locations

Operating system	folder
Unix	~/.aqbanking
Mac OSX	~/.aqbanking
Windows	Documents and Settings/ Username/.aqbanking

Note

On Unix and Mac OSX, these folders will generally not display in the file manager. You must set the file manager to show hidden files and folders to see them.

Tip

On Unix and Mac OSX, the ~ symbol means the home folder.

Putting It All Together

Note

This section begins a tutorial that will continue throughout this book. At the end of each chapter, you will see a Putting It All Together section that walks you through examples to illustrate concepts discussed in that section. Each Putting It All Together section builds on the previous one, so be sure to save your file for easy access.

Let's get started!

1. First, let's create a file to store your real data. Open GnuCash and select File → New File from the *Menubar*. This will start the New Account Hierarchy Setup assistant that allows you to create several accounts at once.

Note

If you are running GnuCash for the first time, you will be presented with the Cannot find default values screen which is described in details in the GnuCash manual.

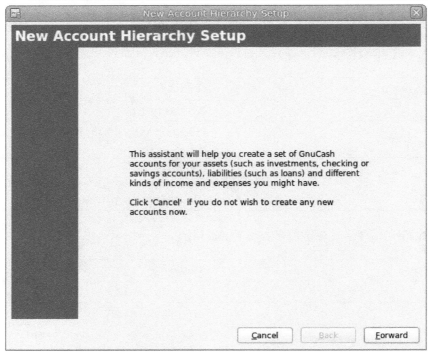

This image shows the first screen of the New Account Hierarchy Setup assistant.

The first screen of the assistant gives you a description of what the assistant does. Click the Forward button to proceed to the next screen.

2. In the second screen, select the currency to use for the new accounts from the dropdown list. Then press the Forward button.

Note

The currency you select here, will be assigned to all the accounts created in this assistant.

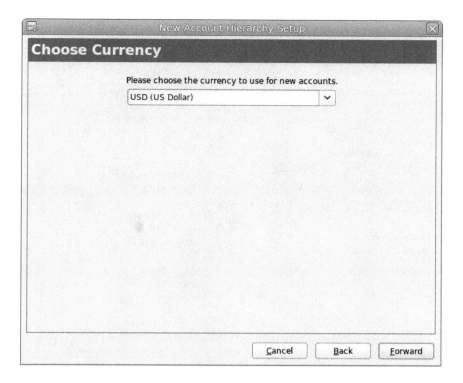

This image shows the second screen of the New Account Hierarchy Setup assistant where you select the currency.

3. In the third screen select the Common Accounts group in the Categories pane. Then press the Forward button to proceed.

Note

If you want, you can select one or more of the predefined account-groups here. For more information on account types, see the section called "GnuCash Accounts".

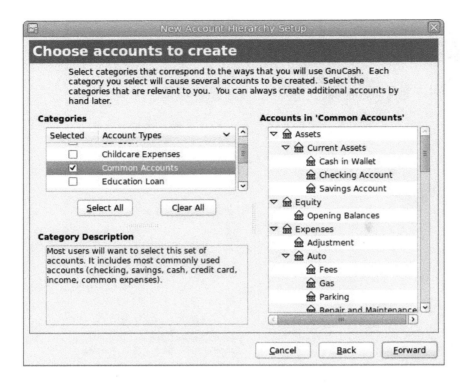

This image shows the third screen of the New Account Hierarchy Setup assistant where you choose the various accounts.

4. In the fourth screen you will be able to set an Opening Balance on each of the accounts, as well as indicate if the account should be a Placeholder. As these features will be described in next chapters, leave all as configured by GnuCash and click Forward to open the last screen of the assistant.

This image shows the fourth screen of the New Account Hierarchy Setup assistant where you can set Opening Balance.

5. In the last screen of the assistant, click Apply to create all the accounts and leave the assistant.

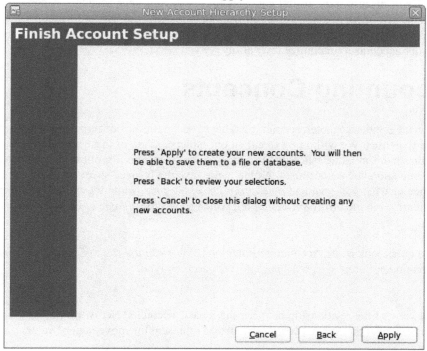

This image shows the last screen of the New Account Hierarchy Setup assistant.

6. After pressing Apply in the previous window, you will be presented with the save dialog. Select the XML Data Format, Name the file as `gcashdata_1`, select the folder where to save the file (remember it as the data file will be used in the tutorials throughout this manual), and finally press the Save as button.

Your main window should now look something like this:

Chapter 3. Accounts

This chapter will discuss some useful concepts for organizing your accounts. Since GnuCash does not impose any specific account tree layout, you are free to design your account structure in any manner you wish. However, there are a few basic accounting concepts which you will probably want to follow when designing your accounts to maximize their utility.

Basic Accounting Concepts

As we saw in the previous chapter, accounting is based on 5 basic account types: Assets, Liabilities, Equity, Income and Expenses. We will now expand on our understanding of these account types, and show how they are represented in GnuCash. But first, let's divide them into 2 groups, the balance sheet accounts and the income and expense accounts. As the name says the balance sheet accounts can be summarized in the balance of what you own and owe *at a point in the time*, while the income and expense accounts can be summarized in the Profit & Loss report, which shows the *change of values in a period of time* like the economic year

Let's have a quick look at the Accounting Equation (*Assets - Liabilities = Equity + (Income - Expenses)*) again as a reminder, before we go deeper into each account type.

A graphical view of the relationship between the 5 basic accounts. Net worth (equity) increases through income and decreases through expenses. The arrows represent the movement of value.

Balance Sheet Accounts

The three so-called *Balance Sheet Accounts* are Assets, Liabilities, and Equity. Balance Sheet Accounts are used to track the things you own or owe.

Assets is the group of things that you own. Your assets could include a car, cash, a house, stocks, or anything else that has convertible value. Convertible value means that theoretically you could sell the item for cash.

Liabilities is the group of things on which you owe money. Your liabilities could include a car loan, a student loan, a mortgage, your investment margin account, or anything else which you must pay back at some time.

Equity is the same as "net worth." It represents what is left over after you subtract your liabilities from your assets. It can be thought of as the portion of your assets that you own outright, without any debt.

Income and Expense Accounts

The two Income and Expense Accounts are used to increase or decrease the value of your accounts. Thus, while the balance sheet accounts simply *track* the value of the things you own or owe, income and expense accounts allow you to *change* the value of these accounts.

Income is the payment you receive for your time, services you provide, or the use of your money. When you receive a paycheck, for example, that check is a payment for labor you provided to an employer. Other examples of income include commissions, tips, dividend income from stocks, and interest income from bank accounts. Income will always increase the value of your Assets and thus your Equity.

Expense refers to money you spend to purchase goods or services provided by someone else *for early consumption*. Examples of expenses are a meal at a restaurant, rent, groceries, gas for your car, or tickets to see a play. Expenses will always decrease your Equity. If you pay for the expense immediately, you will decrease your Assets, whereas if you pay for the expense on credit you increase your Liabilities.

GnuCash Accounts

This section will show how the GnuCash definition of an account fits into the view of the 5 basic accounting types.

But first, let's begin with a definition of an account in GnuCash. A GnuCash account is an entity which contains other sub-accounts, or that contains transactions. Since an account can contain other accounts, you often see account trees in GnuCash, in which logically associated accounts are grouped together within a common parent account.

A GnuCash account must have a unique name (that you assign) and one of the predefined GnuCash "account types". There are a total of 12 account types in GnuCash. These 12 account types are based on the 5 basic accounting types; the reason there are more GnuCash account types than basic accounting types is that this allows GnuCash to perform specialized tracking and handling of certain accounts. There are 6 asset accounts (*Cash, Bank, Stock, Mutual Fund, Accounts Receivable*, and *Other Assets*), 3 liability accounts (*Credit Card, Accounts Payable*, and *Liability*), 1 equity account (*Equity*), 1 income account (*Income*), and 1 expense account (*Expense*).

These GnuCash account types are presented in more detail below.

Balance Sheet Accounts

The first balance sheet account we will examine is *Assets*, which, as you remember from the previous section, refers to things you own.

To help you organize your asset accounts and to simplify transaction entry, GnuCash supports several types of asset accounts:

1. Cash Use this account to track the money you have on hand, in your wallet, in your piggy bank, under your mattress, or wherever you choose to keep it handy. This is the most *liquid*, or easily traded, type of asset.

2. Bank This account is used to track your cash balance that you keep in institutions such as banks, credit unions, savings and loan, or brokerage firms - wherever someone else safeguards your money. This is the second most *liquid* type of account, because you can easily convert it to cash on hand.

3. Stock Track your individual stocks and bonds using this type of account. The stock account's register provides extra columns for entering number of shares and price of your investment. With these types of assets, you may not be able to easily convert them to cash unless you can find a buyer, and you are not guaranteed to get the same amount of cash you paid for them.

4. Mutual Fund This is similar to the stock account, except that it is used to track funds. Its account register provides the same extra columns for entering share and price information. Funds represent ownership shares of a variety of investments, and like stocks they do not offer any guaranteed cash value.

5. Accounts Receivable (A/Receivable) This is typically a business use only account in which you place outstanding debts owed to you. It is considered an asset because you should be able to count on these funds arriving.

Transactions involving an Accounts Receivable account should not be added, changed or deleted in any way other than by using

- post/unpost bill/invoice/voucher or

- process payment

6. Other Assets No matter how diverse they are, GnuCash handles many other situations easily. The group category, "Other Assets", covers all assets not listed above.

   Accounts are repositories of information used to track or record the kinds of actions that occur related to the purpose for which the account is established.

   For businesses, activities being tracked and reported are frequently subdivided more finely than what has been considered thus far. For a more developed treatment of the possibilities, please read the descriptions presented in Chapter 17, *Other Assets* of this Guide.

   For personal finances a person can follow the business groupings or not, as they seem useful to the activities the person is tracking and to the kind of reporting that person needs to have to manage his financial assets. For additional information, consult Chapter 17, *Other Assets* of this Guide.

The second balance sheet account is *Liabilities*, which as you recall, refers to what you owe, money you have borrowed and are obligated to pay back some day. These represent the rights of your lenders to obtain repayment from you. Tracking the liability balances lets you know how much debt you have at a given point in time.

GnuCash offers three liability account types:

1. Credit Card Use this to track your credit card receipts and reconcile your credit card statements. Credit cards represent a short-term loan that you are obligated to repay to the credit card company. This type of account can also be used for other short-term loans such as a line of credit from your bank.

2. Accounts Payable (A/Payable) This is typically a business use only account in which you place bills you have yet to pay.

   Transactions involving an Accounts Payable account should not be added, changed or deleted in any way other than by using

   - post/unpost bill/invoice/voucher or

   - process payment

3. Liability Use this type of account for all other loans, generally larger long-term loans such as a mortgage or vehicle loan. This account can help you keep track of how much you owe and how much you have already repaid.

Tip

Liabilities in accounting act in an opposite manner from assets: *credits* (right-column value entries) increase liability account balances and *debits* (left-column value entries) decrease them. (See note later in this chapter)

The final balance sheet account is *Equity*, which is synonymous with "net worth". It represents what is left over after you subtract your liabilities from your assets, so it is the portion of your assets that you own outright, without any debt. In GnuCash, use this type of account as the source of your opening bank balances, because these balances represent your beginning net worth.

There is usually only a single GnuCash equity account, called naturally enough, Equity. For companies, cooperatives etc. you can create a subaccount for each partner.

Tip

In equity accounts, credits increase account balances and debits decrease them. (See note later in this chapter)

Note

The accounting equation that links balance-sheet accounts is Assets = Liabilities + Equity or rearranged Assets - Liabilities = Equity. So, in common terms, the *things you own* minus the *things you owe* equals your *net worth*.

Income and Expense Accounts

Income is the payment you receive for your time, services you provide, or the use of your money. In GnuCash, use an Income type account to track these.

Tip

Credits increase income account balances and debits decrease them. As described in the section called "Accounting Concepts", credits represent money transferred *from* an account. So in these special income accounts, when you transfer money *from* (credit) the income account to another account, the balance of the income account *increases*. For example, when you deposit a paycheck and record the transaction as a transfer from an income account to a bank account, the balances of both accounts increase.

Expenses refer to money you spend to purchase goods or services provided by someone else. In GnuCash, use an Expense type account to track your expenses.

Tip

Debits increase expense account balances and credits decrease them. (See note later in this chapter.)

Note

When you subtract total expenses from total income for a time period, you get net income. This net income is then added to the balance sheet as retained earnings, which is a type of Equity account.

Below are the standard Income and Expense accounts after selecting Common Accounts in the assistant for creating a new Account Hierarchy (Actions → New Account Hierarchy...).

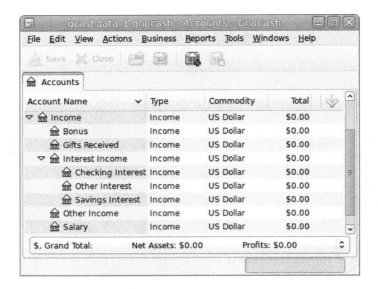

This image shows the standard *Income* accounts

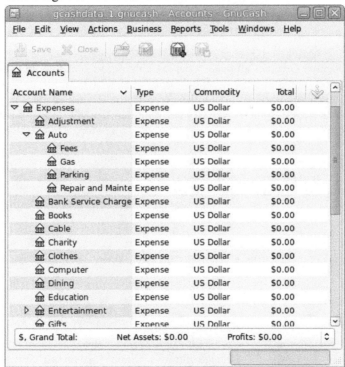

This image shows some standard *Expenses* accounts

Putting It All Together

Let's go through the process of building a common personal finance *chart of accounts* using the information we have learned from this chapter. A chart of accounts is simply a new GnuCash file in which you group your accounts to track your finances. In building this chart of accounts, the first task is to divide the items you want to track into the basic account types of accounting. This is fairly simple, let's go through an example.

Simple Example

Let us assume you have a checking and a savings account at a bank, and are employed and thus receive a paycheck. You have a credit card (Visa), and you pay monthly utilities in the form of rent, phone, and electricity. Naturally, you also need to buy groceries. For now, we will not worry about how much money you have in the bank, how much you owe on the credit card, etc. We want to simply build the framework for this chart of accounts.

Your assets would be the bank savings and checking account. Your liabilities are the credit card. Your Equity would be the starting values of your bank accounts and credit card (we do not have those amounts yet, but we know they exist). You have income in the form of a salary, and expenses in the form of groceries, rent, electricity, phone, and taxes (Federal, Social Security, Medicare) on your salary.

The Basic Top Level Accounts

Now, you must decide how you want to group these accounts. Most likely, you want your *Assets* grouped together, your *Liabilities* grouped together, your *Equity* grouped together, your *Income* grouped together, and your *Expenses* grouped together. This is the most common way of building a GnuCash chart of accounts, and it is highly recommended that you always begin this way.

Start with a clean GnuCash file by selecting File → New File from the menu. The New Account Hierarchy Setup assistant will start. Press Cancel to close the assistant as we don't want to use one of the predefined accounts structure; instead we will build a basic starting account structure from scratch. In the empty GnuCash window select View → New Accounts Page from the menu: the Accounts tab will open. Finally select Actions → New Account....

Now you are ready to build this basic starting account structure

1. Account name Assets (account type Asset, parent account New top level account)

This image shows the dialog to create an assets account

2. Account name Liabilities (account type Liability, parent account New top level account)

3. Account name Equity (account type Equity, parent account New top level account)

4. Account name Income (account type Income, parent account New top level account)

5. Account name Expenses (account type Expenses, parent account New top level account)

When you have created the top-level accounts, the main Account page in GnuCash should look like below.

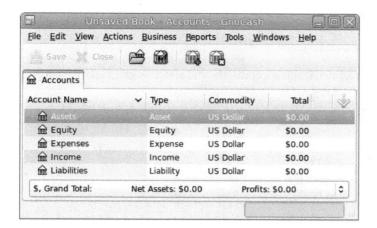

This image shows the basic top-level accounts.

Making Sub-Accounts

You can now add to this basic top-level tree structure by inserting some real transaction-holding sub-accounts. Notice that the tax accounts are placed within a sub-account named *Taxes*. You can make sub-accounts within sub-accounts. This is typically done with a group of related accounts (such as tax accounts in this example).

Tip

Instead of selecting Actions → New Account... from the menu, you can alternatively create a new sub-account of an account by right clicking on the main account's name and selecting the New Account... entry. This will open a dialog similar to the one depicted in the section called "The Basic Top Level Accounts" where the new sub-account will be already set as a child of the main account.

1. Account name Cash (account type Cash, parent account *Assets*)

2. Account name Checking (account type Bank, parent account *Assets*)

3. Account name Savings (account type Bank, parent account *Assets*)

4. Account name Visa (account type Credit Card, parent account *Liabilities*)

5. Account name Salary (account type Income, parent account *Income*)

6. Account name Phone (account type Expense, parent account *Expenses*)

7. Account name Electricity (account type Expense, parent account *Expenses*)

8. Account name Rent (account type Expense, parent account *Expenses*)

9. Account name Groceries (account type Expense, parent account *Expenses*)

10. Account name Taxes (account type Expense, parent account *Expenses*)

11. Account name Federal (account type Expense, parent account *Expenses:Taxes*)

12. Account name Social Security (account type Expense, parent account *Expenses:Taxes*)

13.Account name Medicare (account type Expense, parent account *Expenses:Taxes*)

14.Account name Opening Balance (account type Equity, parent account *Equity*)

After you have created these additional sub-accounts, the end result should look like below

This image shows a simple chart of accounts.

Save this chart of accounts with the name `gcashdata_3`, as well as `gcashdata_3emptyAccts`, as we will continue to use them in the later chapters.

You have now created a chart of accounts to track a simple household budget. With this basic framework in place, we can now begin to populate the accounts with transactions. The next chapter will cover this subject in greater detail.

Chapter 4. Transactions

This chapter will give you the basic information you need to understand and use transactions in GnuCash. Whereas accounts are the framework and structure of a chart of accounts, transactions are the data which fills each account.

Basic Concepts

A *transaction* in a double entry accounting system such as GnuCash is an exchange between at least 2 accounts. Thus, a single transaction must always consist of at least two parts, a *from* and a *to* account. The *from* account is transferring value to the *to* account. Accountants call these parts of a transaction *Ledger Entries*. In GnuCash, they are called *Splits*.

A split identifies the account to which it refers, the amount of money specifically moved to or from that account, and can contain a few other specific pieces of information if needed. GnuCash supports multiple splits in a single transaction, and the splits can move money into or out of the involved accounts arbitrarily.

For example, you receive a paycheck and deposit it into your savings account at the bank. The *transaction* that occurs is that your bank savings account (an asset) received money from your income account. Two accounts are affected, and in this case there is a net increase in your equity.

Working with transactions in GnuCash is performed using what is known as the *account register*. Every account you create has an account register. It will appear familiar to you as it looks very similar to the log used to track checkbooks.

The account register is explained in the upcoming section, the section called "The Account Register".

The Account Register

The *account register* is the GnuCash window, which allows you to view or edit preexisting transactions, or add new transactions for a particular account. To open an account register from the Account Tree, double-click the account name, right click the account name and select Open Account from the menu, or use the Open button on the toolbar. GnuCash will display the account register window.

Features of the Account Register

The *Titlebar* of the account register displays the account name. Below the *Titlebar*, the *Menubar* displays the menu items available within the account register, and the *Toolbar* contains handy buttons that help you work with the account register.

At the bottom left of the register window, GnuCash displays helpful messages as you move about the register. To the right, you can see the current account balance and the total of cleared splits.

Choosing a Register Style

GnuCash offers several options for viewing your registers. The default style is Basic Ledger mode, which displays only the summary of splits affecting the current account. This is the style that most closely resembles other popular personal financial packages. You can choose a different register style from the View menu. There are two other view modes:

- View → Auto-Split Ledger style expands the current transaction automatically. As you highlight a new transaction in the register, the transaction automatically expands to show all splits.

- View → Transaction Journal style shows all splits for all transactions in the register, which is more like an accounting journal.

All styles permit you to view your data in either single-line or double-line format. Select View → Double Line, and you will see your transaction line expand to two register lines. Double-line mode will also display the transaction-level Notes field.

Below are screenshots that demonstrate how the Basic Ledger and Transaction Journal views differ.

For this example, let's assume that you have purchased 3 pair of Jeans for $1,000, and have recorded the purchase as a split transaction with each pair entered on a separate split.

The below screenshots illustrate the different view modes.

First let's view the Jeans transaction from your checking account:

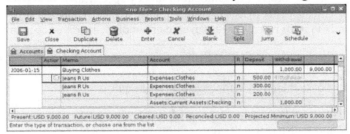

This image shows one split transaction with 3 Jeans purchases

Now, let's open the *Expenses:Clothes* account, and look at it in Basic view.

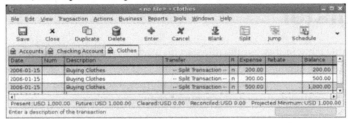

This image shows *Expenses:Clothes* account in Basic Ledger mode.

Three entries appear here, but there was only the single split entry in the checking account. Further examination shows that each row has a different amount, $200, $300, and $500. This demonstrates that each row in this view reflects a single split from the original transaction.

Changing to Transaction Journal mode will display only the original split transaction.

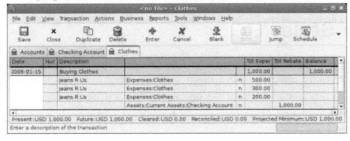

This image shows *Expenses:Clothes* account in Transaction Journal mode.

Using Entry Shortcuts

GnuCash provides several time-saving shortcuts for entering your data. When you type the first few characters of a description that you have used before, the QuickFill feature automatically fills in the rest of the transaction as you last entered it. When you type in the first characters of an account name in either the Transfer field of the transaction line or the Account field of the split line, QuickFill will automatically complete the name from your account list. It also helps you with entering sub-accounts in these fields: simply type the first characters of the parent account name followed by a **:** (colon) and the first characters of the sub-account name. For example, to enter *Assets:Checking*, you might type **A:C** and let GnuCash fill in the rest.

Warning

Because **:** is the account separator symbol, you can not use it in your account names.

Tip

If you really need the colon in your account names, you can select another symbol by Edit → Preferences → Accounts+Character.

Register keyboard shortcuts also save you time, and GnuCash provides several of them. In the date field, you can type:

- + or = to increment the date and - or _ to decrement the date

-] or } to increment the month and [or { to decrement the month

- **M** or **m** to enter the first date of the month

- **H** or **h** to enter the last date of the month

- **Y** or **y** to enter the first date of the year

- **R** or **r** to enter the last date of the year

- **T** or **t** to enter today's date

In the Num field of the transaction line, you can type + to increment the transaction number from the last one you typed in. Typing - will decrement the number. This will also work in the Action field of the split line, if you choose to enter split numbers there. The Action field also supports QuickFill - if you type the first characters of a common action (such as Deposit), GnuCash will fill in the rest.

The Transfer field supports QuickFill of account names. You can start typing an account name and GnuCash will fill in the remaining part of the name. Typing the separator character at any time will complete the current level of the account name, leaving the cursor positioned to start the next level of account name. For example, typing **A:C** the standard set of account names will complete to the *Assets:Checking* account. You can also type the **Menu** or **Ctrl+Down** keys in this field to pop up a list of all account names.

In any of the amount fields, you can use a built-in calculator. Simply type in the first value, followed by +, -, *, or /, then type in the second value. GnuCash will perform the calculation and return the resulting value to the amount field when you press the **Tab** key.

All of the menu items have access keys defined, and these are marked by underlined characters in the menu names. Press **Alt** + [underlined character] to bring up the menu, then select an item by typing its underlined character. For example, typing **Alt+A** brings up the Actions menu, then typing **P** will split the transaction. A few of the menu items also have shortcut keys that immediately invoke the command (typically using the **Ctrl** key). These shortcuts are listed next to the item.

To move around the register, use these keys to save time:

- **Tab** to move to the next field, **Shift+Tab** to move to the previous field

- **Home** to move to the beginning of the field, **End** to move to the end of the field

- **Enter** or ↓ to move to the next transaction, ↑ to move to the previous transaction

- **Page Up** to move up one screen, **Page Down** to move down one screen

- **Shift+Page Up** to go to the first transaction, **Shift+Page Down** to go to the last transaction

In the Reconcile window you can use these keyboard shortcuts:

- **Tab** moves to the next box and **Shift+Tab** moves to the previous box

- Space bar toggles the status between reconciled and not reconciled

- ↑ and ↓ navigate through the entries within the current box

Simple vs. Split Transactions

Every transaction in GnuCash has at least two splits, but a transaction can have more than two splits. A transaction with only two splits is called a *simple transaction*, since it only involves the current account and a single remote account. A transaction with three or more accounts is called a *split transaction*.

When the register is in Basic view, you will see a summary of the splits affecting the current account. For a simple transaction, the Transfer column will display the other account from which money is *transferred*. For a split transaction, the Transfer column will display -- Split Transaction --. You can see the individual splits of each transaction by clicking the Split button in the *Toolbar* while selecting the appropriate transaction.

For split transactions, the first line of the transaction is the *transaction line*. It contains a Date, optional Num (such as a check number), transaction Description, total amount affecting the current account (Tot Deposit here), and updated account Balance after the current transaction. Note that in the expanded view, the Transfer column heading disappears, and there is no account name listed in that field. This line shows you only a summary of the transaction's effect on the current account. For more detailed information, you need to look at the individual splits that make up the transaction.

The partial lines below the transaction line are the *split lines*, and they are separated by gray lines. As you highlight one of the split lines, the column headings change to show the split-related fields:

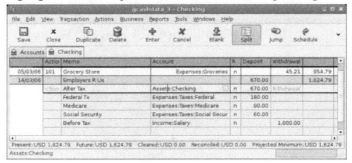

This image shows how split headings change.

Each split contains an optional Action, or type of split, which you can either type in or choose from a pull-down list. The split also contains an optional Memo which describes the split. Each split affects an Account, which can be selected from a pull-down list of your accounts. The R field indicates whether the split has been reconciled. The last two columns show the amount of the split and whether money is coming into or going out of the account.

As we discussed in the section called "Accounting Concepts", total debits (left-column entries) must equal total credits (right-column entries) for each transaction. In the example shown above, the total debits equal the total credits, so this transaction is balanced. If you notice, the transaction line contains the same debit amount as the Checking split line. Why is this shown twice? Because the transaction line is merely a *summary* of the transaction's effect on the current account. The same transaction in a different account will have a different transaction line, one that shows the effect on that particular account. You can see this by highlighting another split line and clicking the Jump button on the *Toolbar*.

In this example, if you jump to the *Income:Salary* account, GnuCash brings up the same transaction in the *Income:Salary* - Register:

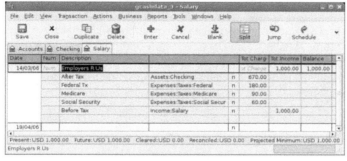

This image shows a jump to the *Income:Salary* account.

Note that the transaction line total now summarizes the effect on the *Income:Salary* account instead of the *Checking Account*, because you are looking at the *Income:Salary* account register. The splits are exactly the same, but the transaction line now reflects the credit to the *Income:Salary* account.

Simple Transaction Example

Starting with the chart of accounts we created in the previous chapter `gcashdata_3`, double click on the Checking asset account. Let's add a simple transaction to the checking account. When you first create your accounts in GnuCash, it is common to start them off with an initial balance.

In the first transaction row, enter a date (eg: March, 1, 2006), a description (eg: "Opening Balance"), click on the Transfer pop-up menu and select *Equity:Opening Balances*, add a deposit value of $1000, and press the **Enter** key. The account register should now appear similar to this figure:

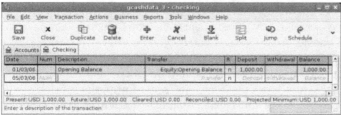

This image shows *Assets:Checking* - Register after inserting a starting value transaction.

Setting the starting balances of an account is an example of a simple two account transaction. In this case, affecting the *Assets:Checking* and the *Equity:Opening Balances* accounts.

As another example of a simple 2 account transaction, add another transaction to describe the purchase of $45.21 worth of groceries. From within the *Assets:Checking* account, you would set Transfer to *Expenses:Groceries*. The account register should now appear:

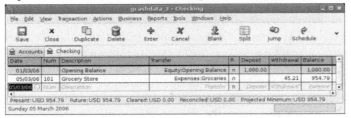

This image shows *Assets:Checking* - Register after adding a transaction for groceries.

Split Transaction Example

The need for 3 or more splits in a transaction occurs when you need to split either the "from" or the "to" account in a transaction into multiple accounts. The classic example of this is when you receive a paycheck. Your take home pay from a paycheck will typically be less than your net pay, with the difference being due to taxes, retirement account payments, and/or other items. Thus, the single transaction of you receiving a paycheck involves other accounts besides simply *Assets:Checking* and *Income:Salary*.

To add the paycheck split transaction from the *Assets:Checking* account register window, click on a new transaction line and click Split. Note that if you have set your register view to Auto-Split or Transaction Journal, the splits will be opened for you. Enter the description of this transaction on the first line(e.g. "Employers R Us"). In the split lines below this, enter the various splits that make up this transaction, one by one. To enter the splits, first choose the account, then enter the amount by which to change the account. Keep in mind that when in an asset account register, amounts entered in the left column increase the account balance, while amounts entered in the right column decrease the balance (for more about this, see the section called "Transactions"). Tab or click the next split line and repeat the process. Note that if you are using the keyboard to navigate the transaction, use **Tab** to move from field to field, as using **Enter** will commit the transaction and create splits to an Imbalance account.

Note

When creating a transaction in GnuCash, splits can be entered in any order. However, when the transaction is closed (either when leaving the transaction, or when pressing the **Enter** key), all debit splits will jump ahead of all credit splits.

In this example, choose the deposit account (*Assets:Checking*) and then enter the amount that is being deposited into it (e.g. $670). Follow this by entering the amounts for the various taxes: *Expenses:Taxes:Federal* account, $180; *Expenses:Taxes:Medicare* account, $90; and *Expenses:Taxes:Social Security* account, $60. Finally, enter the gross total of your paycheck ($1,000 in this example) as a withdrawal transfer from *Income:Salary*.

The final split should look like Figure 4.1, "Entering a split transaction". Remember to press **Enter** after finishing the entry. But you should also know that when you press **Enter**, the split view will be "folded" back into a simplified transaction view. The splits are still there; you just have to click Split to view them. See the section called "Features of the Account Register" for details.

Figure 4.1. Entering a split transaction

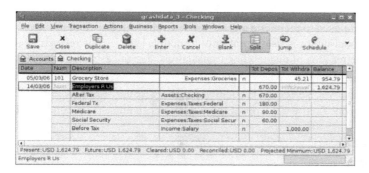

Reconciliation

Once transactions have been entered into GnuCash, it is important to verify that they agree with the records of your financial institution. This verification process is known as **reconciliation**, and it is key to determine whether your records are accurate. Most commonly, you will check transactions against bank statements, although you can use this process to verify any transaction.

GnuCash keeps track of the reconciliation status of each transaction. The reconciliation status of a transaction is shown by the reconciliation R field in a register: y indicates that a transaction has been reconciled, n indicates that it has not, and c indicates that it has been cleared, but not reconciled. A split marked cleared signifies that you got some kind of confirmation that the institution accepted the order (e.g. you have the restaurant's receipt for your credit card purchase). You can toggle the reconciliation status between n and c by clicking in the R field; you can set it to y by using the section called "Reconcile windows".

At the bottom of the account window, there are (among others) two running balances (the cleared and reconciled balance), and the total balance. The former balances should correspond to how much money the bank thinks you have in your account, while the latter includes outstanding transactions.

For example, when you write a check for something, you should enter the transaction into GnuCash. The reconciliation R field of the transaction will initially contain n (new). Your new entry will contribute to the total balance, but not to the cleared and reconciled balance. Later, if you got some confirmation that the check has been cashed, you might click on the transaction's R field to change it to c (cleared). When you do this, the cleared balance will change to include this amount. When the bank statement arrives, you can then compare it to what you've recorded in GnuCash by opening the reconciliation window. There, you will be able to change the R field to y (reconciled).

Note

You cannot reconcile directly in a register window by clicking in the *R* field. You must use the reconciliation window. Once a transaction has been marked *reconciled*, it can no longer be easily changed without breaking the Starting Balance of the next reconciliation.

Warning

It is important to understand that reconciliation is done for a given date, and when you reconcile an account based on a statement from a given date, you are reconciling **all transactions prior to that date**. Therefore, if you add or modify transactions that predate your last reconciliation, your **reconciled** balances will be thrown off.

Reconcile windows

The reconciliation windows are used to reconcile a GnuCash account with a statement that a bank or other institution has sent you. Reconciliation is useful not only to double-check your records against those of your bank, but also to get a better idea of outstanding transactions, e.g. uncashed checks.

To use the reconciliation windows, select an account from the account tree and click on Actions $\rightarrow$ Reconcile. A window like the one below will appear in which you can enter the reconcile information.

The initial reconcile window.

In the initial reconcile window, some Reconcile Information need to be entered.

Statement Date

> The date of the statement you will be reconciling against.
>
> ## Tip
>
> Click on the down arrow in the right of this field to open a calendar

Starting Balance

> This is a non-editable item which displays the balance from the previous reconciliation. It should match the starting balance in your statement.
>
> ## Warning
>
> Sometimes, the opening balance in GnuCash does not match that found on your statement. This can happen the first time you reconcile your account or when a previously-reconciled transaction is de-reconciled or deleted.

Note

The first time you reconcile your account, the starting balance will be 0.00, thus probably not the *opening balance* of your account. When you reconcile the account, the *opening balance* for the account will be included in the reconciliation, and the result should balance.

Tip

In the case when a previously-reconciled transaction is accidentally de-reconciled, you can simply re-reconcile the transaction along with the transactions on the current statement, and the result should balance.

The case of accidentally deleting a previously-reconciled transaction presents more of a challenge; if you cannot determine what was deleted and restore it to the register, you will have to create a dummy transaction to get the reconciliation to finish.

Caution

While the latter case does not matter for your private accounting, you should have a really good explanation for your auditors, if you are the accountant of a club or a company.

Ending Balance

This field should be filled with the ending balance as it appears in the statement.

Note

GnuCash automatically fills this field with the Present balance as shown in the lower part of the account's register.

Include Sub-accounts

Check this option if you want to include in the reconciliation the transactions that belongs to the sub-accounts of the currently selected account.

Enter Interest Payment

Clicking this button opens a new window that allow you to enter an interest transaction to the account to be reconciled.

Tip

The Interest Payment window might be opened automatically when you start a reconciliation for an account of the type *Bank*, *Credit*, *Mutual*, *Asset*, *Receivable*, *Payable*, and *Liability*. If you want to disable this behavior for any of the previous accounts, go to the Register tab of the GnuCash Preferences and uncheck the Automatic interest transfer option. Alternatively, to disable this behavior only for the selected account, press the No Auto Interest Payments for this Account button in the Interest Payment window.

Then, click on the Ok button, and you will see the transactions listing reconcile window:

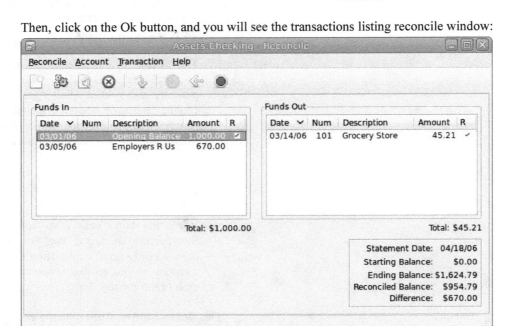

The transactions listing in the reconcile window.

The two panes called Funds In and Funds Out, lists all the unreconciled transactions that belongs to the account that is going to be reconciled. The R columns show whether the transactions have been reconciled.

Now, examine each item on the bank statement, and look for the matching item in the Reconcile window.

If you cannot find a transaction, then perhaps you forgot to enter it, or did not know that the transaction had happened. You can use the New button on the *Toolbar*, or the Transaction → New menu item in the menu, to open a register window and enter the missing transaction. The new item will appear in the Reconcile window when you press the Enter button in the register after entering the transaction.

When you find the item in the Reconcile window, compare the amount in the item to the amount on the statement. If they disagree, you may have made an error when you entered the transaction in GnuCash.

You can use the Edit button on the *Toolbar*, or the Transaction → Edit item, to open a register window and correct the transaction.

If the amounts agree, click on the item in the Reconcile window. A check mark wil appear in the R column aside the selected transaction. GnuCash will automatically update the amounts in the lower right summary pane.

Tip

You can use the **up/down** arrow keys to scroll to the item, the **space** key to mark the item as reconciled and the **Tab** key to switch panes.

You then repeat this for each item that appears on the bank statement, verifying that the amounts match with the amounts in GnuCash, and marking off transactions in GnuCash as they are reconciled.

At the bottom of the Reconcile window there is a Difference field, which should show 0.00 when you are done reconciling. If it shows some other value, then either you have missed transactions, or some amounts may be incorrect in GnuCash. (Or, less likely, the bank may have made an error.)

Note

Under some circumstances, it may be difficult or impossible to determine why an account will not reconcile. If you are unable to correct the discrepancy between your books and a statement, GnuCash includes a Balance button on the *Toolbar* that will automatically create a balancing entry for you in the amount that cannot be reconciled.

To use this, carry out the full reconciliation (marking all transactions that you can identify) and then click this button. GnuCash will create a balancing entry for the remaining discrepancy that uses the *Special Accounts:Orphan-XXX* account (where "XXX" represents your currency). The Reconcile window will close; re-opening it will allow you to check the newly-created balancing entry and finish the process.

When you have marked off all the items on the bank statement and the difference is 0.00, press the Finish button on the *Toolbar* or select Reconcile → Finish from the menu. The Reconcile window will close. In the register window, the R field of the reconciled transactions will change to *y*.

In this case, we have not received all the information yet, so we simply press the Postpone button, so we can continue at a later stage. Observe that the R column indicates we cleared (*c*) two transactions. They have not been reconciled yet, but we have verified these two transactions so they have been marked as cleared. If you look at the *Statusbar* at the bottom of the account register, you will see a summary of what has been reconciled and what has been cleared (Cleared:USD 954.79 Reconciled:USD 0.00)

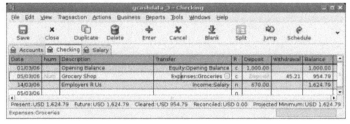

The Checking account after postponing the reconciliation.

Scheduled Transactions

Scheduled transactions are made to help entering repetitive money operations, like subscriptions, insurances or taxes. By using scheduled transactions, you only have to enter the concerned transaction once, set a few parameters like start date, frequency and a little description, and then GnuCash will tell you whenever a scheduled transaction is ready to be created, and create it for you.

In this howto, we'll take a monthly Internet subscription of 20 USD as example, which is taken on the 28th of each month.

In GnuCash, there are two ways of creating scheduled transactions, from the ledger or from the Scheduled Transactions Editor.

Creating from the Ledger

Enter the first occurrence of your to-schedule transaction in the ledger. In the Transfer field for this transaction, type *Expenses:Internet* as shown in the next screenshot.

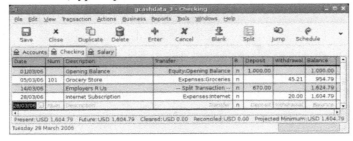

Step one creating scheduled transaction from the ledger

Note

Since we did not create the *Expenses:Internet* account, GnuCash will prompt us to create it.

Then you right click on your transaction and select Schedule...

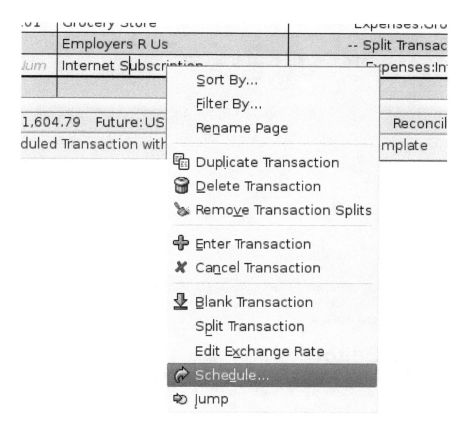

Step two creating scheduled transaction from the ledger

A window like this will appear:

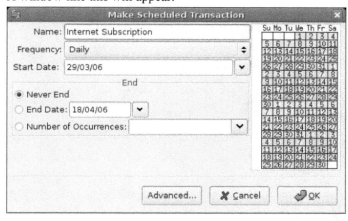

Step three creating scheduled transaction from the ledger

Let's fill the values, we know that the subscription is taken on the 28th each month, and the next one is for next month (since we entered the one for this month manually) :

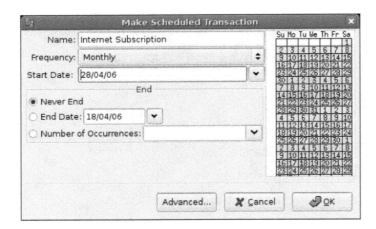

Filling in data to a scheduled transaction

Click the OK button, and the transaction will be scheduled. GnuCash now has memorized this scheduled transaction and on the 28th of next month, it will pop up a window asking if it should create it (see far below for a screenshot of this window).

Creating from the Editor

Another way of entering a scheduled transaction is from the Scheduled Transaction Editor, it may be faster if we have several scheduled transactions to create at once.

From the main accounts windows, select Actions → Scheduled Transactions → Scheduled Transaction Editor from the *Menubar*. A new Scheduled Transactions tab will be opened in the current GnuCash window as shown above:

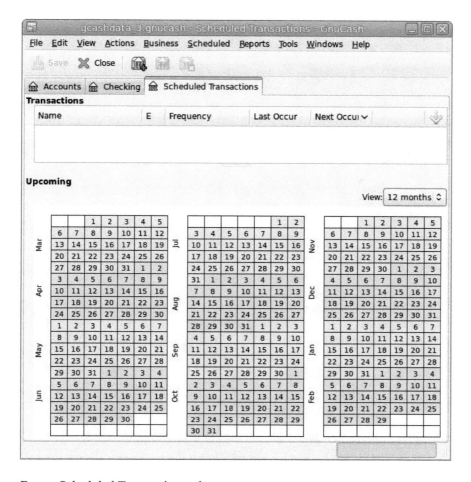

Empty Scheduled Transactions tab

This tab contains a list, now empty, of all the scheduled transactions. Let's create a new one by clicking on the New button in the *Toolbar*. A window like the one below will pop up:

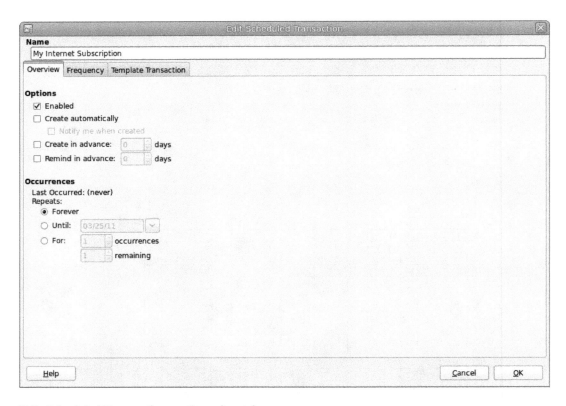

Edit Scheduled Transaction — Overview tab

First, let's enter a name for this new scheduled transaction in the top of the window.

Note

This name will only identify the transaction in the Edit Scheduled Transaction window, it will never appear in the ledger.

In the Options pane of the Overview tab you have four options:

Enable	Sets the status of the scheduled transaction.
Create automatically	If enabled, will insert this transaction in the ledger without asking you before (see below). If needed, you can be advised when the transaction is entered by checking the Notify me when created option.
Create in advance	Sets how many days in advance the transaction will be created.
Remind in advance	Sets how many days in advance a reminder is presented. This can be used, for example, when you have to pay something by check, and a reminder one week before allows you to send your check before the deadline.

The Occurences pane allows you to tell GnuCash that this scheduled transaction won't last for ever. For example if you are repaying a loan, you can enter the loan end date or the number of occurences left.

Select now the Frequency tab in the Edit Scheduled Transaction window. Here you can set the time-related options of the transaction.

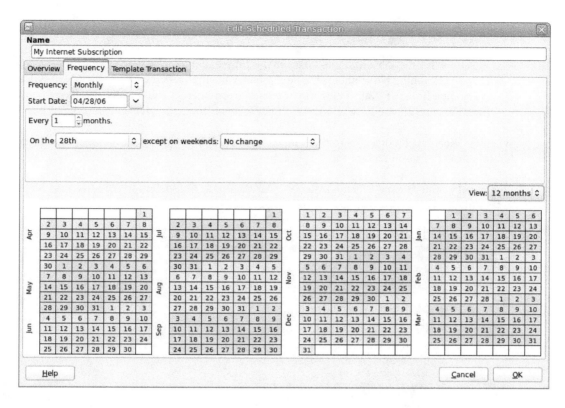

Edit Scheduled Transaction — Frequency tab

Frequency

Sets the basic frequency of the transaction, with options for once, daily, weekly, semi-monthly and monthly. In this example, this is set to monthly.

Note

It is possible to set a transaction to occur at intervals *other* than those listed in the Frequency list, by changing the setting in the Every control (see below).

Start Date

Sets when the transaction will begin. In the example, this would be set to the start of the next month.

Every

This option allows you to schedule transactions by multiplies of the value in Frequency. For example, to create a transaction that runs every 3 weeks, set Frequency to Weeks and Every to 3.

On the and Except on weekends

Sets the day of the month that the transaction is scheduled, and controls what GnuCash will do when the day occurs on a weekend day.

Note

We know that the subscription is taken on the 28th each month, so the Start date will be November 1, 2003 (assuming November is the next month), the Frequency will be Monthly, it will be taken every month on the 28th. Since in our example the internet subscription is automatically taken from the account, we have no need to create it in advance, nor give an end date.

When the elements on this tab are filled in, GnuCash will highlights the calendar below to indicate when future transactions will be run.

Finally select the Template Transaction tab and enter your transaction in the lower part as you would do in the ledger, with the only difference of having no date.

Now, you should have a window like this:

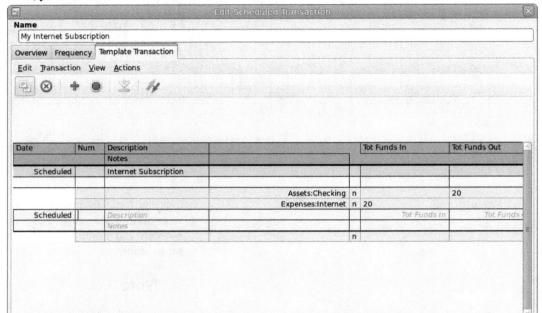

Edit Scheduled Transaction — Template Transaction tab

Remember to click on the Enter icon, to validate and enter the transaction.

Now click OK, it takes you to the Scheduled Transactions tab, now showing one item in the Transactions list:

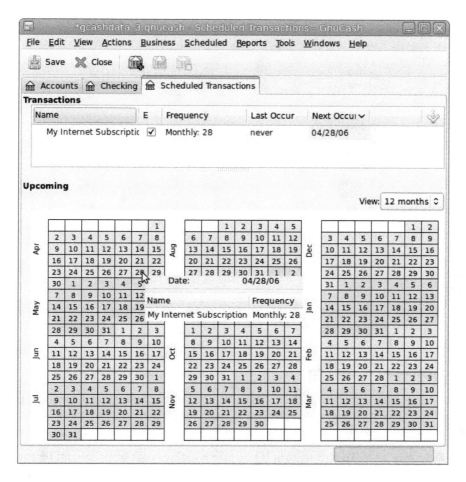

Entered scehduled transaction

Tip

If you click in the calendar part on the first day of one month, a small window, following your mouse, will show you what is planned for this day. To make the small window dissapear again, just click in it one more time.

You can now close the Scheduled Transaction tab, and save your work.

Note

What comes below is just an illustration, and is not meant to be entered into the GnuCash database at this stage. As per this example, the below dialogs will appear when the scheduled transaction is supposed to run.

From now on, when GnuCash is launched and a scheduled transaction is scheduled or need to be entered, you may see a Since Last Run... window summarizing the scheduled transactions operations (Reminder, To-Create etc... a better description of each option can be found in the GnuCash manual):

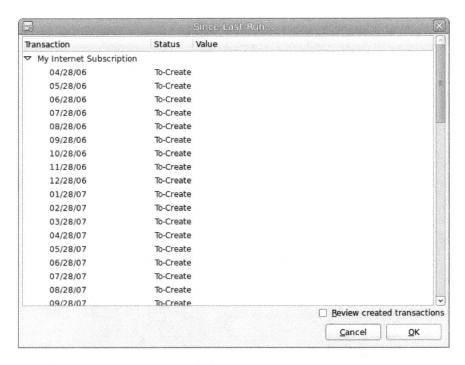

Scheduled transaction popup reminder

You can click on the Status column to change the scheduled transaction status if needed. Then just click on Ok to close the Since Last Run... window and to apply the pending operations. Select Cancel to skip entering in the ledger the pending operations.

If the Status field was set to To-Create, then if you take a look in your bank account register, you'll see the transaction has been created:

Tip

If you enable the Review created transactions option in the lower right of the Since Last Run... window, GnuCash will open, after pressing Ok, the register tab of each account where the scheduled transactions were entered automatically.

Note

If you entered the transaction for 28 of April at this stage, then please *revert back* to the last saved GnuCash file by selecting File → Open and choosing the previously saved gcashdata_3 GnuCash file.

Putting It All Together

In the previous sections of this chapter the concepts and mechanics of working with transactions in GnuCash have been discussed. This section will expand upon the chart of accounts initially built in the previous chapter, by setting some opening balances, adding transactions and a scheduled transaction.

Open GnuCash file

Start with opening the previous datafile we stored, gcashdata_3emptyAccts, and store it as gcashdata_4 directly. The main window should look something like this:

This image shows the starting point for this section.

Opening Balances

As shown earlier with the *Assets:Checking* account, the starting balances in an account are typically assigned to a special account called *Equity:Opening Balance*. To start filling in this chart of account, begin by setting the starting balances for the accounts. Assume that there is $1000 in the savings account and $500 charged on the credit card.

1. Open the *Assets:Savings* account register. Select View from the menu and check to make sure you are in Basic Ledger style. You will view your transactions in the other modes later, but for now let's enter a basic transaction using the basic default style.

2. From the *Assets:Savings* account register window, enter a basic 2 account transaction to set your starting balance to $1000, transferred from *Equity:Opening Balance*. Remember, basic transactions transfer money from a source account to a destination account. Record the transaction (press the **Enter** key, or click on the Enter icon).

3. From the *Assets:Checking* account register window, enter a basic 2 account transaction to set your starting balance to $1000, transferred from *Equity:Opening Balance*.

4. From the *Liabilities:Visa* account register window, enter a basic 2 account transaction to set your starting balance to $500, transferred from *Equity:Opening Balance*. This is done by entering the $500 as a charge in the *Visa* account (or decrease in the *Opening Balance* account), since it is money you borrowed. Record the transaction (press the **Enter** key, or click on the Enter icon).

You should now have 3 accounts with opening balances set. *Assets:Checking*, *Assets:Savings*, and *Liabilities:Visa*.

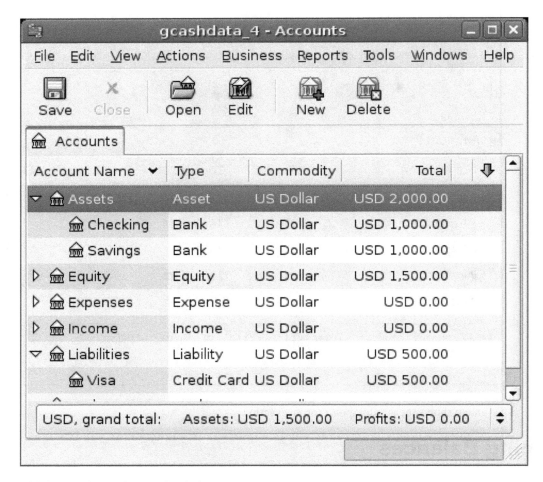

This image shows the opening balances.

Additional Transaction Examples

Now add some more transactions to simulate a month's expenses. During the month, $78 is spent on electricity, $45 on phone, and $350 on rent. All paid by check. We also spent $45.21 on groceries, received $670 as salary, and paid our Internet bill this month. Finally, let's move $100 from the savings account to the checking account.

1. Open the *Expenses:Electricity* account register and enter a simple 2 account transaction to pay the $78 electrical bill at the end of the current month (eg: March 28, 2006). Enter a description (eg: Light Company) and the check number (eg: 102). The Transfer account should be *Assets:Checking*.

2. Open the *Assets:Checking* account register and enter a simple 2 account transaction to pay the $45 phone bill at the end of the current month (eg: March 28, 2006). Enter a description (eg: Phone Company Name) and the check number (eg: 103). The Transfer account should be *Expenses:Phone*. Notice that you can enter expense transactions from either the credit side (the expense accounts) or the debit side (the asset account).

3. Open the *Expenses:Rent* account register and enter a simple 2 account transaction to pay the $350 in rent at the end of the current month (eg: March 28, 2006). Enter a description (eg: April Rent) and the check number (eg: 104). The Transfer account should be *Assets:Checking*.

4. Duplicate this transaction using the Duplicate button in the *Toolbar*. Start by clicking on the current rent transaction, and click on the Duplicate icon. Enter the transaction date a month out in the future

(eg: April 28, 2006), and notice the blue line separator that GnuCash uses to separate future transactions from current ones. In this way, you can enter transactions before they occur.

You could also set up a scheduled transaction to pay your rent, since the value of the rent is likely to be constant for the foreseeable future.

- Start by clicking on the current (April 28) rent transaction, and click on the Schedule icon

- Change to Monthly, change description if needed and press OK

5. To transfer money from your savings account to your checking account, open the *Assets:Savings* account register, add a new transaction setting the Transfer to *Assets:Checking* in the amount of $100 (date 6 March, 2006).

6. As another example of a simple 2 account transaction, add another transaction to describe the purchase of $45.21 worth of groceries on 5 of March. From within the *Assets:Checking* account, you would set Transfer to *Expenses:Groceries*. The account register should now appear:

7. To add a paycheck transaction from the *Assets:Checking* account register window, click on a new transaction line, and click on Split. First enter the description of this transaction on the first line (eg: "Employers R Us"), as well as the date (14 March). In the "split" line below this, enter the deposit into *Assets:Checking* (eg:$670). Follow this with the various tax deposits (*Assets:Checking* (eg: $670), *Expenses:Taxes:Federal* account (eg: $180), *Expenses:Taxes:Medicare* account (eg: $90), and *Expenses:Taxes:Social Security* account (eg: $60)) and lastly the gross total of your paycheck (eg: $1000) as a withdrawal transfer from *Income:Salary*.

8. You also need to pay for your Internet subscription of 20 USD on the 28th.

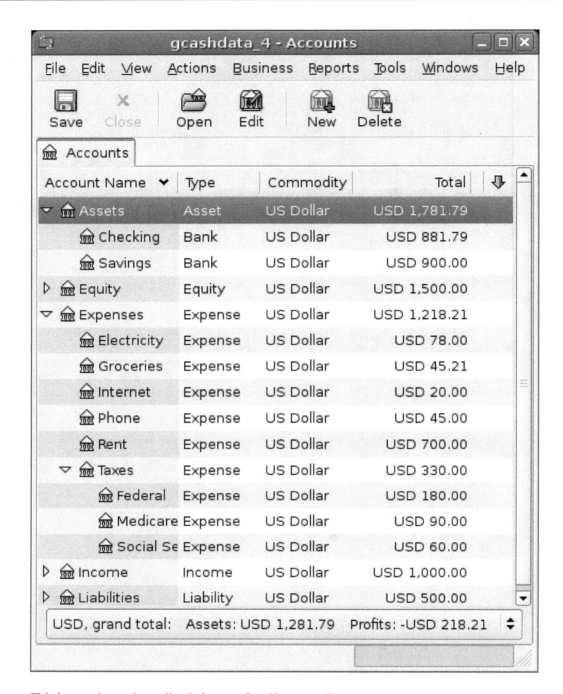

This image shows the ending balances after Chapter 4, *Transactions*.

Save file

Before we go to the report section, let's save the GnuCash data file (gcashdata_4).

Reports

But only having data available on the computer screen will not make your accountant happy, therefore GnuCash comes with a large number of highly customizable reports.

Let's have a look at a Cash Flow, and a Transaction Report.

1. First let's have a look at the Cash Flow report for the month of March.

   Select the cash flow report from Reports → Income & Expense → Cash Flow.

   ## Cash Flow - 01/03/06 to 31/03/06 for
   Selected Accounts

   - Assets
   - Assets:Checking
   - Assets:Savings

Money into selected accounts comes from	
Income:Salary	USD 1,000.00
Money In	**USD 1,000.00**

Money out of selected accounts goes to	
Expenses:Electricity	USD 78.00
Expenses:Groceries	USD 45.21
Expenses:Internet	USD 20.00
Expenses:Phone	USD 45.00
Expenses:Rent	USD 350.00
Expenses:Taxes:Federal	USD 180.00
Expenses:Taxes:Medicare	USD 90.00
Expenses:Taxes:Social Security	USD 60.00
Money Out	**USD 868.21**

Difference	**USD 131.79**

   This image shows the Cash Flow report after Chapter 4, *Transactions*.

   To get this customized report, right click in the report and choose Report Options. Then set the time period, and specify which accounts you want in the report.

2. Now let's have a look at corresponding transaction report for the Checking account.

   Select the transaction report from Reports → Transaction Report.

Transaction Report
From 01/03/06 To 31/03/06

Date	Num	Description	Transfer from/to	Amount
Checking				
05/03/06		Groceries	Groceries	-USD 45.21
06/03/06		Transfer	Savings	USD 100.00
14/03/06		Employers R Us	Split	USD 670.00
28/03/06		Internet subscription	Internet	-USD 20.00
28/03/06	102	Light Company	Electricity	-USD 78.00
28/03/06	103	Phone Company	Phone	-USD 45.00
28/03/06	104	April Rent	Rent	-USD 350.00
Total For Checking				**USD 231.79**
Grand Total				**USD 231.79**

This image shows the Transaction Report for the Checking account during March.

3. Now let's change the transaction report to only show the various Expenses accounts.

Transaction Report
From 01/03/06 To 31/03/06

Date	Num	Description	Transfer from/to	Amount
March 2006				
05/03/06		Groceries	Checking	USD 45.21
14/03/06		Employers R Us	Split	USD 180.00
14/03/06		Employers R Us	Split	USD 90.00
14/03/06		Employers R Us	Split	USD 60.00
28/03/06		Internet subscription	Checking	USD 20.00
28/03/06	102	Light Company	Checking	USD 78.00
28/03/06	103	Phone Company	Checking	USD 45.00
28/03/06	104	April Rent	Checking	USD 350.00
Total For March 2006				**USD 868.21**
Grand Total				**USD 868.21**

This image shows the Transaction Report for the various Expense accounts during March.

Part II. Managing Personal Finances

Table of Contents

Chapter 5. Checkbook

This chapter will give you all the specific information you need to manage your checkbook with GnuCash. Managing your checkbook register is the first step of tracking your finances, and GnuCash makes it much easier to manage than the traditional paper register does.

For one thing, as discussed in Chapter 4, *Transactions*, data entry of common transactions is practically done for you in GnuCash, because of its auto-completion feature. GnuCash keeps a running balance of each account, and it makes reconciling these accounts easy. And the double-entry method helps you account for your spending by requiring a transfer account for withdrawals, so you can easily find out how much money you spend in different areas.

Once you are comfortable with using GnuCash for your checking and other bank accounts, you may wish to continue on with tracking other financial accounts. Chapters 6 through 9 examine methods to manage your other accounts.

Setting up Accounts

The first step in managing your checkbook is to set up the necessary accounts. You can either use the default GnuCash accounts or set up your own. For more detail on how to set up a new account, refer to the section called "The Basic Top Level Accounts". For instructions on importing your accounts from another program, refer to the GnuCash manual.

Let's start with the bank accounts you'll need. You need one GnuCash bank type account for each physical bank account you wish to track. If you are setting up your own accounts or using the default GnuCash accounts, make sure that you have an opening balance transaction for each bank account you own. The easiest way to get this number is to use the balance from your last bank statement as your opening balance. You can enter this in the account information window automatically as part of the New Account Hierarchy Setup assistant, or you can enter a manual transaction directly in the account. To enter the transaction manually, enter a transfer from an Opening Balances account (type equity) to the bank account.

The typical bank accounts you might track include:

- Checking - any institutional account that provides check-writing privileges.

- Savings - an interest-bearing institutional account usually used to hold money for a longer term than checking accounts.

Common transactions that affect these bank accounts are payments and deposits. *Payments* are transfers of money out of the bank account, usually to an expense account. *Deposits* are transfers of money into the bank account, usually from an income account. You will need to set up income and expense accounts to track where that money comes from and where it goes. Remember that a balanced transaction requires a transfer of an equal sum of money from at least one account to at least one other account. So if you deposit money in your checking account, you must also enter the account that money comes from. If you pay a bill from your checking account, you must also enter the account where that money goes.

Entering Deposits

Most deposit transactions are entered as a transfer from an income account to a bank account. Income may come from many sources, and it's a good idea to set up a separate income type account for each different source. For example, your income may come mainly from your paychecks, but you may also receive interest on your savings. In this case, you should have one income account for salary and another income account for interest income.

Tip

Be sure to check the Tax-Related box and assign an appropriate tax category in the Income Tax Information Dialog (Edit → Tax Report Options) when you set up taxable income accounts. Some types of income, such as gift income, may not be considered taxable, so check the appropriate tax rules to determine what is taxable. For ways to track capital gains income, refer to Chapter 9, *Capital Gains*.

Before you start entering paycheck deposits, decide how much detail you want to track. The basic level of detail is to enter your net pay, just like you would in your paper register. This is easiest, but you can get even more information out of GnuCash if you enter your gross pay with deductions. It takes a bit more effort to enter the deductions, but entering your tax withholding information throughout the year allows you to run useful tax status reports in GnuCash at any time. These reports can help you determine whether you are withholding enough tax, and they can help you estimate your tax bill ahead of time. If you are unsure about the level of detail, start by entering net pay. You can always go back and edit your transactions later if you decide you want more detail.

Entering Withdrawals

When you withdraw money from your bank account, for whatever reason, you are transferring money from your bank account to some other location. In GnuCash, this other location is tracked as an account. The more detailed accounts you create and use for your spending, the more information you will get about where your money goes.

Withdrawals take many forms. ATM withdrawals are one of the most common transactions. Writing checks is one way to withdraw money to pay bills, to buy purchases, or to give to charity. Depending on your bank, you might also have service charges, where the bank withdraws the money from your account. Transfers of money out to another account are also withdrawals. We will take a look at each of these types of withdrawals and how to record them in GnuCash.

ATM/Cash Withdrawals

Cash withdrawals are handled as a transfer from a bank account to a cash account. GnuCash provides special *Cash* type accounts for tracking your cash purchases, so you should set up a cash account to record your ATM and other cash withdrawals.

Cash accounts can be used for different levels of detail. On a basic level of detail, you simply transfer money to it from your checking account. That tells you how much money you took out of checking on a given day, but it doesn't tell you where that cash was spent. With a little more effort, you can use the cash account to record your cash purchases as well, so that you can see where that cash went. You record these purchases as a transfer from the cash account to expense accounts.

Some people record every cash purchase, but this takes a lot of work. An easier way is to record the purchases for which you have receipts, but then adjust the balance of the account to match what is in your wallet.

It's a good idea to at least set up a cash account for your withdrawals. Then if you decide to track where your cash goes, you can enter transactions for the money you spend. You determine what level of detail you want to use.

Reconciling Your Accounts

GnuCash makes reconciliation of your bank account with your monthly bank statement much easier. the section called "Reconciliation" gives instructions on how to reconcile your transactions with the monthly bank statement. This is the main reconciliation task that should be done every month.

But what about all those other accounts you created? Should those be reconciled too? If you receive a statement for the account, then you should consider reconciling that account. Examples include the checking account statement, the savings account statement, and the credit card statement. Credit card statements and credit card transactions are covered in the Chapter 6, *Credit Cards*, so if you are interested in tracking your credit cards in GnuCash, take a look at the instructions provided there.

Income and expense accounts are usually not reconciled, because there is no statement to check them against. You also don't need to reconcile cash accounts, for the same reason. With a cash account, though, you might want to adjust the balance every once in a while, so that your actual cash on hand matches the balance in your cash account. Adjusting balances is covered in the next section.

Putting It All Together

In Chapter 4, *Transactions*, you entered some transactions in your checking account. In this chapter, we will add more transactions and then reconcile them.

Opening Balances

So, let's get started by opening the gcashdata file you saved in the last chapter (`gcashdata_4`). Your chart of accounts should look like this:

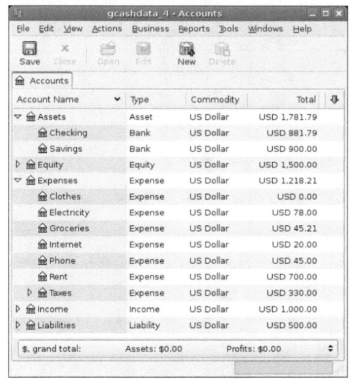

This image shows the Chart of Accounts.

Add some transactions

1. Now open the *Checking* account from the main window. In the last chapter, you entered some paycheck transactions as deposits into Checking. Now we will enter another kind of deposit - a transfer of money from Savings into Checking. On a blank line, enter a transaction to transfer $500 from *Savings* to *Checking* (In this case, the last transaction date was March 28, but this transfer transaction took place on the March 24). Your Transfer account will be *Savings*, since you are in the *Checking* account. Your *Checking* account should now look like this:

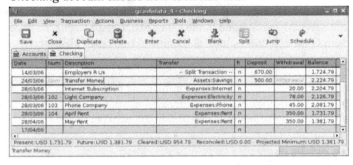

This image shows the Checking Account Register.

2. Now let's write some checks on this account. First, write a check to HomeTown Grocery for $75 (5th of March). Your transfer account is *Groceries*, since all of this money is going to buy groceries. Next, write a check to ABC Hardware for $100 (6 of March), and split this amount between two expenses: *Household* $50 and *Tools* $50. You will need to create an *Expense* type account for each of these, then enter splits for them. Your checking account should now look like this;

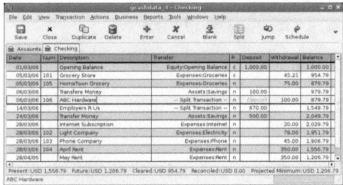

This image shows the Checking Account Register after registering some more checks.

3. Suppose you now need to withdraw some money. You don't have a cash account set up in your chart of accounts, so you will need to create one. Create the account as Cash as a top-level account of type Asset. From your *Checking* account register, enter an ATM type withdrawal to transfer $100 from *Checking* to *Cash* on the 25 of March.

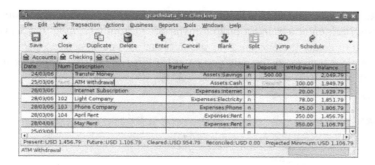

This image shows the Checking Account Register with an ATM withdrawal.

Opening Balances

Now we are ready to reconcile this *Checking* account, using this sample bank statement:

Date	Description	Decreasing	Increasing	Balance
1/03/2006	Starting Balance			1,000.00
5/03/2006 Check:101:Grocery Store		45.21		954.79
6/03/2006 Transfer			100.00	1,054.79
8/03/2006 Check:106:ABC Hardware		100.00		954.79
14/03/2006 Salary			670.00	1,624.79
15/03/2006 Check:105:HomeTown Grocery		75.00		1,549.79
24/03/2006 Transfer			500.00	2,049.79
25/03/2006 ATM		100.00		1,949.79
28/03/2006 Check:102:Light Company		78.00		1,871.79
28/03/2006 Check:103:Phone Company		45.00		1,826.79
28/03/2006 Check:104:Apartment 4 Rent		350.00		1,476.79
28/03/2006 Best Internet		20.00		1,456.79
31/03/2006 Service Charge		5.00		1,451.79
31/03/2006	Ending Balance			1,451.79

This image shows a sample Bank Statement.

1. Select Actions → Reconcile from the menu, and fill in the Closing balance as $1451.79. Click OK to begin reconciling the account. Check off the entries as they appear on the sample statement. When you have checked off all your entries, the reconcile window should look like this:

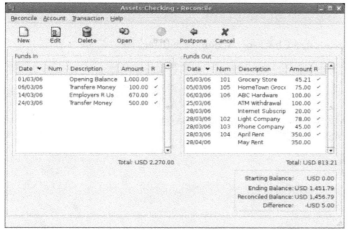

This image shows the reconcile window with a $5 difference.

Notice that your reconciled balance differs from your ending balance by $5.00. If you look at the sample bank statement, you will see there is a $5.00 service charge that has not been added to your *Checking* account.

2. So click on the *Checking* register and add the $5.00 service charge to your *Checking* account. On a blank line of the *Checking* register, enter a transaction to transfer $5.00 from *Checking* to a *Service Charges* account. (You will need to create the *Service Charges* account as type Expense.) Use the transaction date printed on the sample statement as the date you enter for this transaction. Your *Checking* account should now look like this:

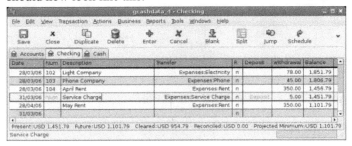

This image shows the Checking Account Register with service charge added.

3. Click back on the Reconcile window, and you should see the service charge now under Funds Out. Click on it to mark it as reconciled, and note that the difference amount below now becomes 0.00. Click the Finish button on the *Toolbar* to complete the reconciliation. The Reconcile R column in your *Checking* register should now show y for each transaction you just reconciled. Also observe the bottom status row that now indicates Reconciled: USD 1451.79

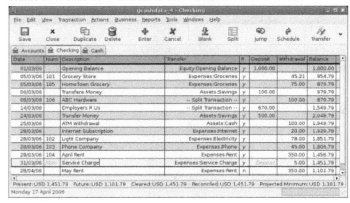

This image shows the reconciled Checking Account Register.

Save file

Go back to the main window and save your file with the new `gcashdata_5` name. Your chart of accounts is steadily growing, and it should now look like this:

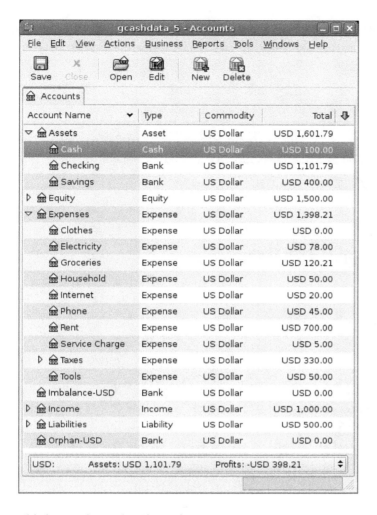

This image shows the Chart of Accounts.

Reports

As we did in the previous chapter, let's have a look at a Cash Flow, and a Transaction Report.

1. First let's have a look at the Cash Flow report for the month of March.

   Select the cash flow report from Reports → Income & Expense → Cash Flow.

Cash Flow - 01/03/06 to 31/03/06 for

Selected Accounts

- Assets:Cash
- Assets:Checking
- Assets:Savings

Money into selected accounts comes from	
Equity:Opening Balance	USD 2,000.00
Income:Salary	USD 1,000.00
Money In	**USD 3,000.00**

Money out of selected accounts goes to	
Expenses:Electricity	USD 78.00
Expenses:Groceries	USD 120.21
Expenses:Household	USD 50.00
Expenses:Internet	USD 20.00
Expenses:Phone	USD 45.00
Expenses:Rent	USD 350.00
Expenses:Service Charge	USD 5.00
Expenses:Taxes:Federal	USD 180.00
Expenses:Taxes:Medicare	USD 90.00
Expenses:Taxes:Social Security	USD 60.00
Expenses:Tools	USD 50.00
Money Out	**USD 1,048.21**

Difference	**USD 1,951.79**

This image shows the Cash Flow report after Chapter 5, *Checkbook*.

2. Now let's have a look at corresponding transaction report for the various Asset accounts.

Select the transaction report from Reports → Transaction Report.

Transaction Report
From 01/03/06 To 31/03/06

Date	Num	Description	Transfer from/to	Amount
Cash				
25/03/06		ATM Withdrawal	Checking	USD 100.00
Total For Cash				**USD 100.00**
Checking				
01/03/06		Opening Balance	Opening Balance	USD 1,000.00
05/03/06	101	Grocery Store	Groceries	-USD 45.21
05/03/06	105	HomeTown Grocery	Groceries	-USD 75.00
06/03/06		Transfere Money	Savings	USD 100.00
06/03/06	106	ABC Hardware	Split	-USD 100.00
14/03/06		Employers R Us	Split	USD 670.00
24/03/06		Transfer Money	Savings	USD 500.00
25/03/06		ATM Withdrawal	Cash	-USD 100.00
28/03/06	102	Light Company	Electricity	-USD 78.00
28/03/06	104	April Rent	Rent	-USD 350.00
28/03/06		Internet Subscription	Internet	-USD 20.00
28/03/06	103	Phone Company	Phone	-USD 45.00
31/03/06		Service Charge	Service Charge	-USD 5.00
Total For Checking				**USD 1,451.79**
Savings				
01/03/06		Opening Balance	Opening Balance	USD 1,000.00
06/03/06		Transfere Money	Checking	-USD 100.00
24/03/06		Transfer Money	Checking	-USD 500.00
Total For Savings				**USD 400.00**
Grand Total				**USD 1,951.79**

This image shows the Transaction Report for the Assets accounts during March.

3. Now let's change the transaction report to only show the various *Expenses* account.

Transaction Report

From 01/03/06 To 31/03/06

Date	Num	Description	Account	Amount
05/03/06	101	Grocery Store	Groceries	USD 45.21
05/03/06	105	HomeTown Grocery	Groceries	USD 75.00
06/03/06	106	ABC Hardware	Household	USD 50.00
06/03/06	106	ABC Hardware	Tools	USD 50.00
14/03/06		Employers R Us	Federal	USD 180.00
14/03/06		Employers R Us	Social Security	USD 60.00
14/03/06		Employers R Us	Medicare	USD 90.00
28/03/06		Internet Subscription	Internet	USD 20.00
28/03/06	104	April Rent	Rent	USD 350.00
28/03/06	102	Light Company	Electricity	USD 78.00
28/03/06	103	Phone Company	Phone	USD 45.00
31/03/06		Service Charge	Service Charge	USD 5.00

| Grand Total | | | | **USD 1,048.21** |

This image shows the Transaction Report for the various Expense accounts during March.

Notice that you have not yet used one of the accounts listed in your chart, the Credit Card account. Now that you know how to keep track of your bank and cash accounts in GnuCash, you may want to start tracking your credit cards as well. GnuCash provides a special type of account for credit cards, and this is discussed in the next chapter.

Chapter 6. Credit Cards

This chapter will show you how to manage your credit cards using GnuCash.

Concepts

Since you probably write a check or make an electronic payment to the credit card company each month, you may think of your credit card bill as an expense - but it really is not an expense. Why? A credit card account is a short-term loan - you buy things on that loan account, and then you eventually have to pay back the money, often with interest (your finance charge). The purchases you make with that credit card are your expenses.

You have a couple of options when entering credit card transactions, so choose the one that fits your desired level of detail. The simplest method is to simply track monthly payments to the credit card company. From your bank account, you enter a transfer of money each month to the credit card expense account. This will show you the amount of money you are paying each month to the credit card company, but it won't show you any information about your credit card balance or credit card purchases.

A more complete way to track your credit card in GnuCash is to enter each purchase and payment as a separate transaction. Using the credit card account register, you enter your receipts throughout the month. When your credit card statement arrives, you reconcile the credit card account to the statement, and you enter your payment as a transfer of money from your checking account to your credit card account. This method gives you more information about your balance during the month and points out any discrepancies during reconciliation, but you will have to do more data entry.

Setting Up Accounts

To begin managing your credit cards in GnuCash, you should set up a Liability top level account and under this parent account create credit card type accounts for each credit card you use. If you are tracking only the payments you make to the credit card company, then all you need is a bank account and a credit card account to enter your transactions.

The charges you make on your credit card are expenses, so you will have to set up these accounts under the top-level account called Expenses. If you decide to keep a more detailed records of your purchases, you will need to create expense accounts for each kind of purchase you make. Since you will also be reconciling the balance to your credit card statements, you should also enter an opening balance in each credit card account. The easiest way to do this is to use your last statement balance as the opening balance.

Simple Setup

If you do not want to track each expense made on the credit card, you can set up a simple account hierarchy like this:

-Assets
 -Bank
-Liabilities
 -Credit Card
-Expenses
 -Credit Card

In this example, if you enter your total amount charged per month as a transaction between *Liabilities:Credit Card* and *Expenses:Credit Card*. When you make a payment, you would enter a transaction between *Assets:Bank* and *Liabilities:Credit Card*.

The obvious limitation of this simple credit card setup is that you cannot see where your money is going. All your credit card expenses are being entered in the Credit Card expense account. This is, however, very simple to set up and maintain.

Complete Setup

If you want to track your expenses more completely, you should set up multiple expense accounts named for the various kinds of expenses you have. Each charge on your credit card is then entered as a separate transaction between your Credit Card liability account and a specific expense account. Below is an example of an account hierarchy for this:

```
-Assets
  -Bank
-Liabilities
  -Credit Card
-Expenses
  -Food
  -Car
  -Clothes
  -Entertainment
  -Interest
  -Service
```

Clearly, you should enter specific expense accounts which fit your spending habits. The only difference with this setup as compared to the simple setup is that the expenses have been subdivided by groups. Also notice that there is an "Interest" expense, this is used for when your credit card charges interest on your monthly unpaid balance. The "Service" expense account is used to track service expenses associated with the credit card, such as the yearly usage fee if it exists. With this setup, you will be able to see where your money goes every month, grouped according to the expense accounts.

The rest of this chapter will assume you are using the complete setup.

Entering Charges

Entering your charges provides you with a more complete picture of your spending habits. Charges on a credit card are tracked as a transaction between the credit card liability account and the appropriate expense account.

When you pay for goods or services with your credit card, you are telling the credit card company to pay the merchant for you. This transaction will increase the amount of money you owe the credit card company, and the credit card balance will increase. The other side of these transactions will in most cases be an expense account. For example, if you buy clothing from a store with your credit card for $50, you would be transferring that money from the credit account into Expenses:Clothing.

Entering these transactions into GnuCash allows you to track how much you owe the credit card company, as well as provides you a better picture of your overall accounts. It also allows you to monitor your account and ensure that fraud is avoided.

Adding transactions to a credit card account is similar to entering transactions in other accounts. You can enter them manually, or import them from your credit card company using a compatible import format.

For assistance with entering transactions, see Chapter 6 of the Help manual and Chapter 4, *Transactions*.

Entering Payments

Most payments to your credit card bill are entered as transfers from a bank account (asset) to the credit card account (liability). When you pay the monthly bill, you are withdrawing money from a bank account to pay down the credit card balance. This transaction decreases both your bank account balance and the amount of credit card debt you owe.

When you return a purchase, you receive a refund on your credit card. This is another type of payment in that it decreases the amount of credit card debt you owe. If you recorded the original purchase transaction as a transfer from the credit card account to the expense, you now simply reverse that transaction: transfer the money back from the expense to the credit card account. This transaction decreases both the expense account balance and the credit card account balance. For example, if you originally recorded a credit card purchase of clothing, the transaction is a transfer from the credit card account to the clothing expense account. If you then return that clothing for a refund, you simply transfer the money back from the clothing expense account to the credit card account.

Note

A common mistake is to enter a refund as income. It is not income, but rather a "negative expense". That is why you must transfer money from the expense account to your credit card when you receive a refund.

To clarify this, let's run through an example. You bought some jeans for $74.99 on your VISA card, but realized one day later that they are too big and want to return them. The shop gracefully agrees, and refunds your credit card.

1. Start with opening the previous datafile we stored (gcashdata_5), and store it as gcashdata_6.

2. Open the *Liabilities:Visa* account register and enter a simple 2 account transaction to pay the $74.99 jeans purchase. The Transfer account should be *Expenses:Clothes* and you Charge your *Visa* account with the $74.99.

Note

Since we had not created the *Expenses:Clothes* account previously, GnuCash will prompt us to create it. Just remember to create it as an Expense account

3. Enter the refund in one of the following way.

- Enter the same transaction as the purchase transaction, but instead of a "Charge" amount, use a "Payment" amount in the Credit Card account register.

- Select the purchase transaction you want to refund (that is the Jeans transaction in our case), and selecting Transaction → Add Reversing Transaction. Modify the date as needed.

After reversing the transaction, your credit card account should look something like this:

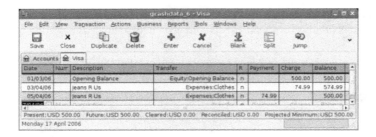

This image shows *Liability:Credit Card* - Register after reversing a purchase transaction.

And the *Expenses:Clothes* register should look something like this:

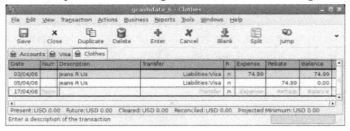

This image shows *Expenses:Clothes* register after reversing a purchase transaction.

4. Save the GnuCash data file.

Putting It All Together

Now that we have covered the basic ideas behind the various transactions you must make to successfully track your credit card in GnuCash, let's go through an example. In this example, we will make credit card purchases, refund two of the purchases, get charged interest on the unpaid balance, reconcile the credit card account, and finally make a partial payoff of the credit card.

Open GnuCash file

Start with opening the previous datafile we stored, gcashdata_5, and store it as gcashdata_6 directly. The main window should look something like this:

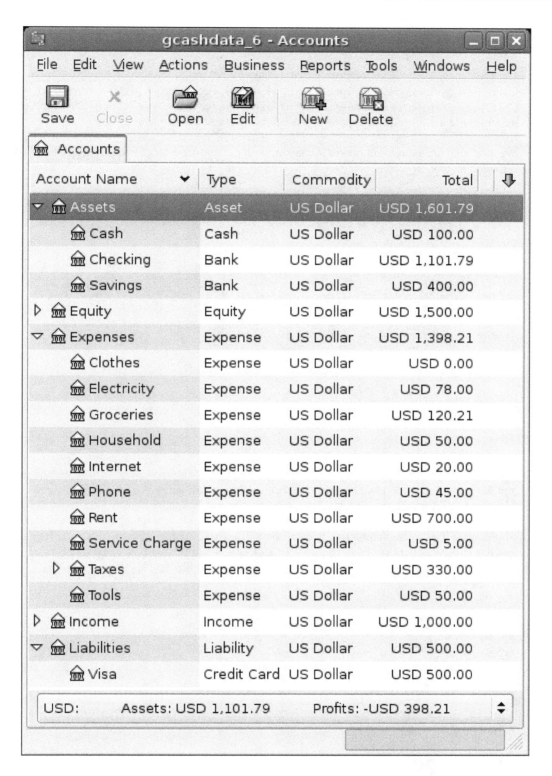

Starting account structure for tracking a credit card in the putting it all together example.

Purchases

Let's make some purchases on our visa card. Start by buying $25 worth of food from the Greasy Spoon Cafe, $100 worth of clothing from Faux Pas Fashions, $25 worth of gasoline from Premium Gasoline, $125 worth of groceries and household items from Groceries R Us (split between $85 in groceries and $40 in household items) and finally, $60 worth of household items from CheapMart.

We also redo the exercise in previous chapter, with purchasing a pair of Jeans for $74.99 on April 3, and refund them two days later.

The register window for the credit card liability should look like this:

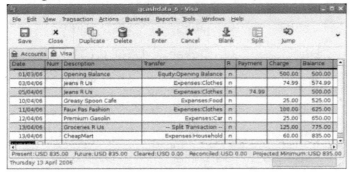

Initial credit card purchases.

Refund

Now suppose that on April 15th you return the clothes you bought on April 11th from Faux Pas Fashions and they give you credit back on your credit card. Enter a transaction for the credit card refund for the full $100 amount. Remember to use the same transfer account you used for the original purchase, and enter the amount under the Payment column. GnuCash will automatically complete the name and transfer account for you, but it will also automatically enter the $100 in the Charge column. You will need to reenter the amount in the Payment column. The transaction looks like this:

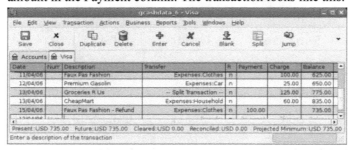

Returning clothes to Faux Pas Fashions, refund to credit card.

Interest Charge

After the month of spending, unfortunately, the credit card bill arrives in the mail or you access it on-line through the internet. You have been charged $20 in interest on the last day of April because of the balance you carried from the previous month. This gets entered into the credit card account as an expense.

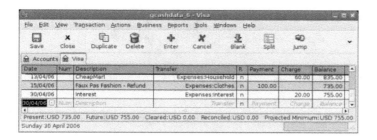

Interest charge.

Reconciliation

When your credit card bill arrives you should reconcile your credit card account to this document. This is done using GnuCash's built-in reconciliation application. Highlight the credit card account and click on Actions → Reconcile.... This reconciliation procedure is described in detail in the the section called "Reconciliation", but we will step through the process here as well. For this example, let's assume that the credit card statement is dated May 1st, with a final balance of $455. Enter these values in to the initial Reconcile window as shown here.

Initial account reconciliation window.

During the reconciliation process, you check off each transaction in the account as you confirm that the transaction appears in both your GnuCash account and the credit card statement. For this example, as shown in the figure below, there is a $300 difference between your GnuCash accounts and the credit card statement.

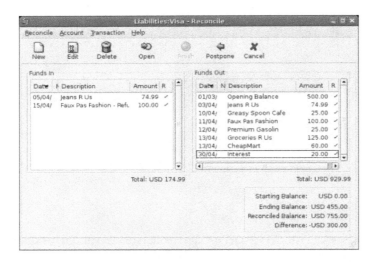

Main account reconciliation window, demonstrating a discrepancy of $300.

Some investigation uncovers that you forgot to record a payment you made on March 5th to the credit card company for $300, you must enter this payment transaction from your bank account to the credit card. Now the credit card statement and your GnuCash account can be reconciled, with a balance of $455.

Payment

Assuming you have completed reconciliation of your credit card account, you need to make a payment to the credit card company. In this example, we owe $455 but will make a partial payment of $300 again this month. To do so, enter a transaction from your bank account to the credit card account for $300, which should reduce your credit card balance to $155. Your credit card account register should now appear like this:

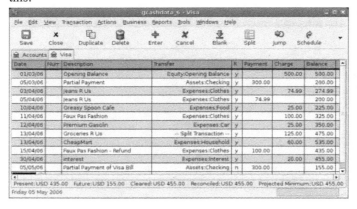

Account register after account reconciliation and payment.

Go back to the main window and save your file (gcashdata_6). Your chart of accounts is steadily growing, and it should now look like this:

GnuCash Chart of Accounts after account reconciliation and payment.

Save file

Last, save the GnuCash data file (`gcashdata_6`).

Reports

As we did in the previous chapters, let's have a look at a Cash Flow, and a Transaction Report.

1. First let's have a look at the Cash Flow report for the liability account Visa during the month of March.

   Select the cash flow report from Reports → Income & Expense → Cash Flow.

   ## Cash Flow - 01/03/06 to 30/04/06 for

   Selected Accounts

   ● Liabilities:Visa

Money into selected accounts comes from	
Assets:Checking	USD 300.00
Expenses:Clothes	USD 174.99
Money In	**USD 474.99**

Money out of selected accounts goes to	
Equity:Opening Balance	USD 500.00
Expenses:Car	USD 25.00
Expenses:Clothes	USD 174.99
Expenses:Food	USD 25.00
Expenses:Groceries	USD 85.00
Expenses:Household	USD 100.00
Expenses:Interest	USD 20.00
Money Out	**USD 929.99**

Difference	-USD 455.00

   This image shows the Cash Flow report after Chapter 6, *Credit Cards*.

2. Now let's have a look at corresponding transaction report for the Visa account.

   Select the transaction report from Reports → Transaction Report.

Transaction Report

From 01/03/06 To 30/04/06

Date	Num	Description	Transfer from/to	Amount
Visa				
March 2006				
01/03/06		Opening Balance	Opening Balance	USD 500.00
05/03/06		Partial Payment	Checking	-USD 300.00
Total For March 2006				**USD 200.00**
April 2006				
03/04/06		Jeans R Us	Clothes	USD 74.99
05/04/06		Jeans R Us	Clothes	-USD 74.99
10/04/06		Greasy Spoon Cafe	Food	USD 25.00
11/04/06		Faux Pas Fashion	Clothes	USD 100.00
12/04/06		Premium Gasolin	Car	USD 25.00
13/04/06		Groceries R Us	Split	USD 125.00
13/04/06		CheapMart	Household	USD 60.00
15/04/06		Faux Pas Fashion - Refund	Clothes	-USD 100.00
30/04/06		Interest	Interest	USD 20.00
Total For April 2006				**USD 255.00**
Total For Visa				**USD 455.00**
Grand Total				**USD 455.00**

This image shows the Transaction Report for the Visa account during March/April.

3. Now let's change the transaction report to only show the various Expenses accounts.

Transaction Report
From 01/04/06 To 30/04/06

Date	Num	Description	Account	Amount
Car				
12/04/06		Premium Gasolin	Car	USD 25.00
Total For Car				**USD 25.00**
Clothes				
03/04/06		Jeans R Us	Clothes	USD 74.99
05/04/06		Jeans R Us	Clothes	-USD 74.99
11/04/06		Faux Pas Fashion	Clothes	USD 100.00
15/04/06		Faux Pas Fashion - Refund	Clothes	-USD 100.00
Total For Clothes				**USD 0.00**
Food				
10/04/06		Greasy Spoon Cafe	Food	USD 25.00
Total For Food				**USD 25.00**
Groceries				
13/04/06		Groceries R Us	Groceries	USD 85.00
Total For Groceries				**USD 85.00**
Household				
13/04/06		Groceries R Us	Household	USD 40.00
13/04/06		CheapMart	Household	USD 60.00
Total For Household				**USD 100.00**
Interest				
30/04/06		Interest	Interest	USD 20.00
Total For Interest				**USD 20.00**
Rent				
28/04/06		May Rent	Rent	USD 350.00
Total For Rent				**USD 350.00**
Grand Total				**USD 605.00**

This image shows the Transaction Report for the various Expense accounts during April.

Chapter 7. Loans

This chapter explains how to manage your loans with GnuCash.

Basic Concepts

A loan is defined as a financial transaction in which someone pays for the use of someone else's money. There are many familiar examples of loans: credits cards, auto loans, house mortgages, or a business loan.

Terminology

Before discussing tracking loan in GnuCash specifically, it will be helpful to present a glossary of terminology. The terms presented below represent some of the basic concepts found concerning loans. It is a good idea to become familiar with these terms, or at least, refer back to this list if you encounter an unfamiliar word in the later sections.

- *Amortization* - the repayment plan which will insure that a loan is eventually paid off, typically utilizing equal valued monthly payments. These payments are usually split into principal and interest, where the amount of principal per payment increases (and interest decreases) as the amortization period elapses.

- *Borrower* - the person or company that receives the money from a loan.

- *Default* - when a borrower fails to repay a loan according to the terms agreed upon with the lender.

- *Deferment* - a temporary delay in the repayment of a loan.

- *Delinquency* - is the term that refers to late payments.

- *Disbursement* - amount of the loan paid to the borrower. Some loans have multiple disbursements, meaning the borrower does not receive the full amount of the loan at one time.

- *Interest* - the expense charged by the lender to the borrower for the use of the money loaned. This is typically expressed in terms of a yearly percentage charged on the principal borrowed, known as the *Annual Percentage Rate* or APR.

- *Lender* - the company or person who lends money to a borrower.

- *Loan Fee* - a processing fee removed from the principal at the time the borrower receives a loan.

- *Principal* - the original amount of the loan, or the amount of the original loan that is still owed. When you make a monthly payment on a loan, part of the money pays the interest, and part pays the principal.

- *Promissory Note* - the legal agreement between the borrower and lender concerning the loan.

Setting Up Accounts

When a borrower obtains a loan, it is usually with the intention to make a purchase of something of value. In fact, most loans require the borrower to buy some predetermined asset, such as a house. This asset is insurance against the borrower defaulting on the loan. There are, of course, examples of loans which do not necessarily have an associated high value asset, such as educational loans.

For the account structure presented here, we will assume the loan was used to purchase a compensating asset.

A loan is a liability, the interest you accrue on the loan is an on-going expense, and any administrative fees you may have to pay would be another expense. The thing purchased with the money from a loan is an asset. With these parameters, we can now present a basic loan account structure:

Basic Loan Account Structure

-Asset
    -Current Assets
        -Savings Account
    -Fixed Assets
        -Asset Purchased
-Liability
    -Loans
        -Mortgage Loan
-Expenses
    -Interest
        -Mortgage Interest
    -Mortgage Adm Fees

GnuCash has a number of predefined loan account hierarchies available, including Car Loans and Home Mortgage Loans. To access these predefined account structures, click on Actions → New Account Hierarchy... and select the loan types in which you are interested.

Calculations

Determining loan amortization schedules, periodic payment amounts, total payment value, or interest rates can be somewhat complex. To help facilitate these kinds of calculations, GnuCash has a built-in Loan Repayment Calculator. To access the calculator, go to Tools → Loan Repayment Calculator.

The GnuCash Loan Repayment Calculator.

The Loan Repayment Calculator can be used to calculate any one of the parameters: Payment Periods, Interest Rate, Present Value, Periodic Payment, or Future Value given that the other 4 have been defined. You will also need to specify the compounding and payment methods.

• *Payment Periods* - the number of payment periods.

- *Interest Rate* - the nominal interest rate of the loan, ie: the yearly interest rate.

- *Present Value* - the present value of the loan, ie: current amount owed on the loan.

- *Periodic Payment* - the amount to pay per period.

- *Future Value* - the future value of the loan, ie: the amount owed after all payment periods are over.

- *Compounding* - two interest compounding methods exist, discrete or continuous. For discrete compounding select the compounding frequency from the popup menu with a range from yearly to daily.

- *Payments* - the popup menu allows you to select the payment frequency with a range from yearly to daily. You can also select whether your payments occur at the beginning or end of the period. Payments made at the beginning of the payment period have interest applied to the payment as well as any previous money paid or money still owed.

Example: Monthly Payments

What is your monthly payment on a $100000 30 year loan at a fixed rate of 4% compounded monthly?

This scenario is shown in the example image above. To perform this calculation, set Payment Periods to 360 (12 months x 30 years), Interest Rate to 4, Present Value to 100000, leave Periodic Payment empty and set Future Value to 0 (you do not want to owe anything at the end of the loan). Compounding is Monthly, Payments are Monthly, assume End of Period Payments, and Discrete Compounding. Now, click on the Calculate button next to the Periodic Payment area. You should see $-477.42.

Answer: You must make monthly payments of 477.42.

Example: Length of Loan

How long will you be paying back a $20000 loan at 10% fixed rate interest compounded monthly if you pay $500 per month?

To perform this calculation, leave Payment Periods empty, set Interest Rate to *10*, Present Value to *20000*, Periodic Payment is *-500*, and Future Value is *0* (you do not want to owe anything at the end of the loan). Compounding is *Monthly*, Payments are *Monthly*, assume End of Period payments, and Discrete Compounding. Now, click on the Calculate. You should see 49 in the Payment Periods field.

Answer: You will pay off the loan in 4 years and 1 month (49 months).

Advanced: Calculation Details

In order to discuss the mathematical formulas used by the Loan Repayment Calculator, we first must define some variables.

n == number of payment periods
%i == nominal interest rate, NAR, charged
PV == Present Value
PMT == Periodic Payment
FV == Future Value
CF == Compounding Frequency per year

PF == Payment Frequency per year

Normal values for CF and PF are:
  1   == annual
  2   == semi-annual
  3   == tri-annual
  4   == quaterly
  6   == bi-monthly
  12 == monthly
  24 == semi-monthly
  26 == bi-weekly
  52 == weekly
  360 == daily
  365 == daily

Converting between nominal and effective interest rate

When a solution for n, PV, PMT or FV is required, the nominal interest rate (i) must first be converted to the effective interest rate per payment period (ieff). This rate, ieff, is then used to compute the selected variable. When a solution for i is required, the computation produces the effective interest rate (ieff). Thus, we need functions which convert from i to ieff, and from ieff to i.

To convert from i to ieff, the following expressions are used:
Discrete Interest: $ieff = (1 + i/CF)^{\wedge}(CF/PF) - 1$
Continuous Interest: $ieff = e^{\wedge}(i/PF) - 1 = exp(i/PF) - 1$

To convert from ieff to i, the following expressions are used:
Discrete Interst: $i = CF*[(1+ieff)^{\wedge}(PF/CF) - 1]$
Continuous Interest: $i = ln[(1+ieff)^{\wedge}PF]$

Note

NOTE: in the equations below for the financial transaction, all interest rates are the effective interest rate, "ieff". For the sake of brevity, the symbol will be shortened to just "i".

The basic financial equation

One equation fundamentally links all the 5 variables. This is known as the fundamental financial equation:

$PV*(1 + i)^{\wedge}n + PMT*(1 + iX)*[(1+i)^{\wedge}n - 1]/i + FV = 0$

Where: X = 0 for end of period payments, and
        X = 1 for beginning of period payments

From this equation, functions which solve for the individual variables can be derived. For a detailed explanation of the derivation of this equation, see the comments in the file src/calculation/fin.c from the GnuCash source code. The A, B, and C variables are defined first, to make the later equations simpler to read.

$A = (1 + i)^{\wedge}n - 1$

$B = (1 + iX)/i$

$C = PMT*B$

$n = ln[(C - FV)/(C + PV)]/ln((1 + i)$

$PV = -[FV + A*C]/(A + 1)$

$PMT = -[FV + PV*(A + 1)]/[A*B]$

$FV = -[PV + A*(PV + C)]$

The solution for interest is broken into two cases.

The simple case for when PMT == 0 gives the solution:

$i = [FV/PV]^{\wedge}(1/n) - 1$

The case where PMT != 0 is fairly complex and will not be presented here. Rather than involving an exactly solvable function, determining the interest rate when PMT !=0 involves an iterative process. Please see the src/calculation/fin.c source file for a detailed explanation.

Example: Monthly Payments

Let's recalculate the section called "Example: Monthly Payments", this time using the mathematical formulas rather than the Loan Repayment Calculator. What is your monthly payment on a $100000 30 year loan at a fixed rate of 4% compounded monthly?

First, let's define the variables: n = (30*12) = 360, PV = 100000, PMT = unknown, FV = 0, i = 4%=4/100=0.04, CF = PF = 12, X = 0 (end of payment periods).

The second step is to convert the nominal interest rate (i) to the effective interest rate (ieff). Since the interest rate is compounded monthly, it is discrete, and we use: ieff = $(1 + i/CF)^{\wedge}(CF/PF)$ - 1, which gives ieff = $(1 + 0.04/12)^{\wedge}(12/12)$ - 1, thus ieff = 1/300 = 0.0033333.

Now we can calculate A and B. A = $(1 + i)^{\wedge}n$ - 1 = $(1 + 1/300)^{\wedge}360$ - 1 = 2.313498. B = (1 + iX)/i = (1 + (1/300)*0)/(1/300) = 300.

With A and B, we can calculate PMT. PMT = -[FV + PV*(A + 1)]/[A*B] = -[0 + 100000*(2.313498 + 1)] / [2.313498 * 300] = -331349.8 / 694.0494 = -477.415296 = -477.42.

Answer: You must make monthly payments of 477.42.

House Mortgage (How-To)

A house mortgage can be setup using the account structure present in the section called "Setting Up Accounts".

As an example, assume you have $60k in you bank account, and you buy a $150k house. The mortgage is charging 6% APR, and has administrative fees (closing costs, etc) of 3%. You decide to put $50k down, and thus will need to borrow $103k, which will give you $100 after the closing costs are paid (3% of $100k).

Your accounts before borrowing the money:

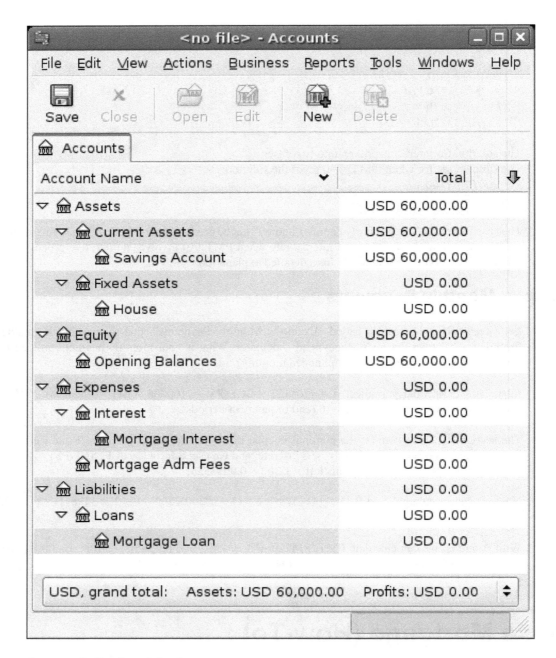

Accounts Before Receiving Loan

The purchase of the house is recorded with a split transaction in the *Assets:House* account, with $50k coming from the bank (IE: your down payment), and $100k coming from the Mortgage. You can place the $3k closing costs in the same split, and we increase the house loan to $103k to include the closing costs as well.

Table 7.1. Buying a House Split Transaction

Account	Increase	Decrease
Assets:Fixed Assets:House	$150,000	
Assets:Current Assets:Bank		$50,000

Liabilities:Loans:Mortgage Loan		$103,000
Expenses:Mortgage Adm Fees	$3000	

The split will look like this in the *Assets:Fixed Assets:House* Account:

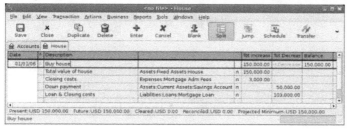

Mortgage Split Transaction

Which will give a Chart of Accounts like this:

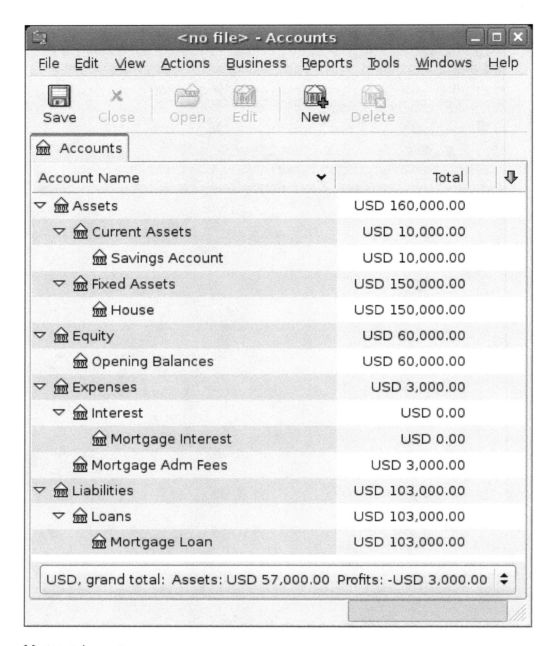

Mortgage Account

A Personal Loan to a friend (How-To)

It is not always you are borrowing money from the bank, sometimes you borrow money from your family, or perhaps even lend money to a friend. This How-To chapter will describe one way to handle lending money to a friend.

We are basing this How-To on the following generic account structure.

```
-Asset
  -Bank
    -Bank Account
```

-Money owed to you
   -Person
-Income
  -Interest Income
   -Person

This example will show how to track a personal loan of 2,000 USD (default currency) to your friend Peter

Loan Specifications

Peter wants to borrow $2,000 dollars from you and plans to pay you back monthly for the next 18 months. Since he is your friend, (but not that close) you both agree on a yearly interest rate of 5%.

In summary we have the below details. Peter's loan details:

- Pinciple Amount - $2,000

- Term - 18 months with 12 payments per year

- Annual Percentage Rate: 5%

- Monthly Payment : ??

So how do you calculate the Monthly Payment?

You have a number of different options, like paper and pen, Linux Calculator, Open Office's Calc module, but the easiest is to use GnuCash Loan Repayment Calculator. This tells you that the Monthly Payment should be $115.56.

But you need to know how much of this is Interest and how much is Principal to be able to do a proper bookkeeping. For this you need a more powerful tool, something like the Calc module in OpenOffice.org, and in particular the PMT function.

			Start Amount	Interest	Principal	End Amount
		Jan	2,000.00	8.33	107.23	1,892.77
Loan Amount	$2,000.00	Feb	1,892.77	7.89	107.67	1,785.10
Number of months	18	Mar	1,785.10	7.44	108.12	1,676.97
Payments per year	12	Apr	1,676.97	6.99	108.57	1,568.40
Interest per year	5%	May	1,568.40	6.54	109.03	1,459.37
Monthly payment	$115.56	Jun	1,459.37	6.08	109.48	1,349.89
		Jul	1,349.89	5.62	109.94	1,239.96
		Aug	1,239.96	5.17	110.39	1,129.56
Monthly Payment=PMT(C8/C7,C6,-C5,0)		Sep	1,129.56	4.71	110.85	1,018.71
		Oct	1,018.71	4.24	111.32	907.39
Interest=($C$8/$C$7)*F4		Nov	907.39	3.78	111.78	795.61
		Dec	795.61	3.32	112.25	683.37
Principal=$C$9-G4		Jan	683.37	2.85	112.71	570.65
		Feb	570.65	2.38	113.18	457.47
End Amount=F4-H4		Mar	457.47	1.91	113.65	343.81
		Apr	343.81	1.43	114.13	229.69
		May	229.69	0.96	114.60	115.08
		Jun	115.08	0.48	115.08	-0.00
		Total		$80.10	$2,000.00	

Detailed view over the private loan to Peter

Accounts for the loan

Let's start with the following accounts (all accounts have the same currency, in this case USD)

Assets:Bank:USD
Assets:Money owed to you:Peter
Income:Interest Income:Peter
Equity:Opening Balances:USD

Lending the money

When you have lent money to your friend, you have in fact moved money from an Asset account (like Bank, Checking or similar) to your Asset account *Money owed to you*. To record this you enter the following transaction into the *Assets:Money owed to you:Friend* account.

Table 7.2. Personal loan to a Friend

Account	Increase	Decrease
Assets:Money owed to you:Friend	$2,000	
Assets:Bank:USD		$2,000

Chart of Accounts after lending money

Receiving first payment

When the first payment ($115.56) is received, you will need to determine how much is for the principal loan, and how much is for the loan interest.

- Outstanding loan amount this period = $2,000

- Payment per month = $115.56

- Payment breakdown

- 5%/12 * $2,000 = $8.33 Interest

- $115.56 - $8.33 = $107.23 Principal

This can be translated to the following GnuCash entry

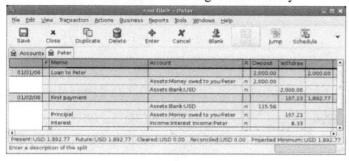

Detailed view over first payment

The balance on Peter's loan is now $2,000 - $107.23 = $1,892.77

Receiving second payment

When the second payment ($115.56) is received, you will again need to determine how much is for the principal loan, and how much is for the loan interest.

- Outstanding loan amount this period = $1,892.77

- Payment per month = $115.56

- Payment breakdown

- 5%/12 * $1,892.77 = $7.89 Interest

- $115.56 - $7.89 = $107.67 Principal

This can be translated to the following GnuCash entry

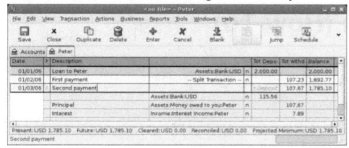

Detailed view over the second payment

The balance on Peter's loan is now $1,892.77 - $107.67 = $1,785.10

The Chart of accounts looks now like this

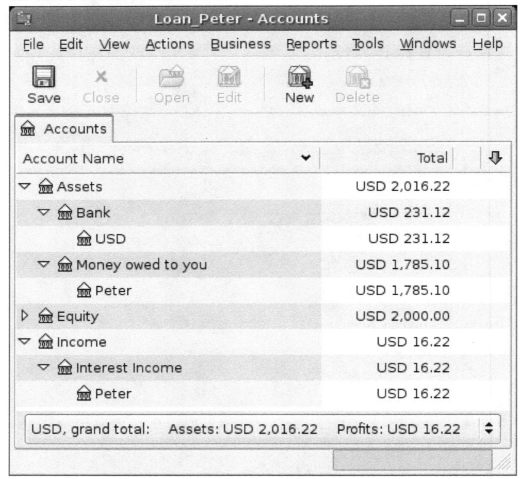

Chart of Accounts after second payment

As you can see, the interest varies for every month, as well as the principal amount. So for every payment you receive you need to calculate the proper amounts for your various split entries.

The interest amount will be less and less for every payment (since it is calculated on a smaller loan amount all the time), until the last payment where it is more or less 0. Please review the Figure of Detailed view over private loan to Peter for more details

Automobile Loan (How-To)

The Automobile Loan, or in common terms, Car Loan, is treated more or less exactly as the House loan. The only difference is different accounts, and different interest rates.

Basic Car Loan Account Structure

```
-Asset
  -Current Assets
    -Savings Account
  -Fixed Assets
    -Car
```

```
-Liability
 -Loans
    -Car Loan
-Expenses
 -Interest
    -Car Loan Interest
 -Car Loan Adm Fees
```

For more information, please check the section called "House Mortgage (How-To)"

Reconciling with the Loan Statements (How-To)

Reconciling a loan statement is no different from reconciling a bank or credit card statement.

During the period you should have recorded all the various loan related transactions, and every one of them are touching the Liability:Loans:*Loan* account. For instance, paying off a bit of the loan decreases your *Bank Account,* and increases the *Loan account, Loan Interest* as well as perhaps *Loan administration fee.*

With the loan statement in your hands, open the Loan account, start the reconcile assistant, and tick of all the various transaction you have recorded. When you have finished, the reconciling difference should be 0, and if it is not, then you will have to go through the account and compare it with the loan statement to find the difference. When you have reached a 0 in difference, then your loan account is reconciled and you can finish the Reconcile assistant.

For more information on how to Reconcile, please check the section called "Reconciliation"

Selling a house or a car (How-To)

When you will record the selling of your house in GnuCash you have some different options. Here we will go through two of them, one in which you only recorded the purchase amount, and now the selling amount. The other where you have followed the ups and downs on the property market and registered various Unrealized gains over the time.

Simple Transaction

In this way you only record the proper sale amount.

Let's work through two samples of selling a house, one with a profit, and one with a loss. If you want to sell a car instead, just substitute the house account with a car account.

```
-Assets
 -Fixed Assets
  -House
 -Current Assets
  -Saving
-Income
 -Capital Gains Long
  -House
```

- You bought a house for $300,000 once upon a time, and now managed to sell it for $600,000. How do you record this?

To record this you need to increase our bank account with the $600k, and decrease some other accounts with $600k. The house account only contains $300k which is what you bought it for, so you move this amount to your bank account. That means you are lacking $300k. This amount you fetch from the *Income:Captial Gains Long:House* account. The split transaction you enter into your *bank* account (*Assets:Current Assets:Saving*) should look like this.

Table 7.3. Selling an asset (house) with a profit

Account	Increase	Decrease
Assets:Current Assets:Saving	$600,000	
Assets:Fixed Assets:House		$300,000
Income:Capital Gains Long:House		$300,000

- You bought a house for $300,000 once upon a time, but due to a newly created airport, could only sell it for $230,000. How do you record this?

To record this you need to increase your bank account with the $230k, and decrease some other accounts with $230k. The house account contains $300k which is more than what you sold it for. So let's move $230k of it to your bank account. After this you have $70k remaining in your house account which needs to be removed. You move it to our *Income:Capital Gains Long:House* account, which will indicate a loss. The split transaction you enter into your *house* account (*Assets:Fixed Assets:House*) should look like this.

Table 7.4. Selling an asset (house) with a loss

Account	Increase	Decrease
Assets:Fixed Assets:House		$300,000
Assets:Current Assets:Saving	$230,000	
Income:Capital Gains Long:House	$70,000	

A More Complex Transaction

In this example, we will touch a little on some more complicated accounting principles. For more details on this subject, please check Chapter 9, *Capital Gains*

Here we will only touch on the case when you have accurately estimated the current value of your house. For the other cases (over-, and under-estimated), please check Chapter 9, *Capital Gains*.

```
-Assets
  -Fixed Assets
    -House
      -Cost
      -Unrealized Gain
  -Current Assets
    -Saving
-Income
```

-Realized Gain
   -House
-Unrealized Gain
   -House

You bought a house for $300,000 once upon a time, and over the years kept a close look on the market and updated your records with the estimated current value of your house. At the time you want to sell it, you have determined that the current market value is $600,000.

The difference between $600,000 (estimated market value) and $300,000 (purchase value) is the current Unrealized Gain value. Therefore you have a total of $300,000 in your *Assets:Fixed Assets:House:Unrealized Gain* account

How do you record this sell transaction?

To record this you need to increase your bank account with the $600k, and decrease some other accounts with $600k. You must first change from unrealized gain to realized gain for your *Income* accounts. Lastly you need to transfer the full amounts from the *Assets:Fixed Assets:House* sub-accounts.

The transaction you enter into your *Income:Realized Gain:House* account account should look like this.

Table 7.5. Selling an asset (house) with a profit

Account	Increase	Decrease
Income:Realized Gain:House	$300,000	
Income:Unrealized Gain:House		$300,000

The transaction you enter into your *Assets:Current Assets:Saving* account should look like this.

Table 7.6. Selling an asset (house) with a profit 2

Account	Increase	Decrease
Assets:Current Assets:Saving	$600,000	
Assets:Fixed Assets:House:Cost		$300,000
Assets:Fixed Assets:House:Unrealized Gain		$300,000

After having recorded these transactions you see that your House Asset have a value of 0, your Savings account have increased with $600,000, and lastly, the *Income:Realized Gain* have increased to $300,000.

Chapter 8. Investments

This chapter explains how to manage your investments with GnuCash. Most people have an investment plan, whether its just putting money into a CD account, investing through a company sponsored plan at your workplace or buying and selling stocks and bonds through a brokerage. GnuCash gives you tools to help you manage these investments such as the *Price Editor* which allows you to record changes in the prices of stocks you own.

Basic Concepts

An investment is something that you purchase in the hopes of generating income, or that you hope to sell in the future for more than you paid. Using this simple definition, many things could be considered investments: the house you live in, a valuable painting, stocks in publicly traded companies, your savings account at the bank, or a certificate of deposit. These many types of investments will be discussed in this chapter in terms of how to track them using GnuCash.

Terminology

Before discussing investments specifically, it will be helpful to present a glossary of investment terminology. The terms presented below represent some of the basic concepts of investing. It is a good idea to become familiar with these terms, or at least, refer back to this list if you encounter an unfamiliar word in the later sections.

Capital gains	It is the difference between the purchase and selling prices of an investment. If the selling price is lower than the purchase price, this is called a *capital loss*. Also known as *realized gain/loss*.
Commission	It is the fee you pay to a broker to buy or sell securities.
Common stock	It is a security that represents a certain fractional ownership of a company. This is what you buy when you "buy stock" in a company on the open market. This is also sometimes known as *capital stock*.
Compounding	It is the concept that the reinvested interest can later earn interest of its own (interest on interest). This is often referred to as *compound interest*.
Dividends	Dividends are cash payments a company makes to shareholders. The amount of this payment is usually determined as some amount of the profits of the company. Note that not all common stocks give dividends.
Equities	Equities are investments in which the investor becomes part (or whole) owner in something.

This includes common stock in a company, or real estate.

Interest

It is what a borrower pays a lender for the use of their money. Normally, this is expressed in terms of a percentage of the principal per year. For example, a savings account with 1% interest (you are the lender, the bank is the borrower) will pay you $1 for every $100 you keep there per year.

Liquidity

It is a measure of how easily convertible an investment is to cash. Money in a savings account is very liquid, while money invested in a house has low liquidity because it takes time to sell a house.

Principal

It is the original amount of money invested or borrowed.

Realized vs Unrealized Gain/Loss

Unrealized gain or loss occurs when you've got a change in price of an asset. You realize the gain/loss when you actually sell the asset. See also *capital gain/loss*.

Return

It is the total income plus capital gains or losses of an investment. See also *Yield*.

Risk

It is the probability that the return on investment is different from what was expected. Investments are often grouped on a scale from low risk (savings account, government bonds) to high risk (common stock, junk bonds). As a general rule of thumb, the higher the risk the higher the possible return.

Shareholder

Shareholder is a person who holds common stock in a company.

Stock split

It occurs when a company offers to issue some additional multiple of shares for each existing stock. For example, a "2 for 1" stock split means that if you own 100 shares of a stock, you will receive an additional 100 at no cost to you. The unit price of the shares will be adjusted so there is no net change in the value, so in this example the price per share will be halved.

Valutation

It is the process of determining the market value or the price the investment would sell at in a "reasonable time frame".

Yield

It is a measure of the amount of money you earn from an investment (IE: how much income you receive from the investment). Typically this is reported as a percentage of the principal amount. Yield does not include capital gains or loses (see Return). Eg: A stock sells for $100 and gives $2 in dividends per year has a yield of 2%.

Types of Investments

Below is presented some of the broad types of investments available, and examples of each type.

- *Interest-bearing account or instrument*

This type of investment usually allows you immediate access to your money, and will typically pay you interest every month based on the amount of money you have deposited. Examples are bank savings accounts (and some interest bearing checking accounts) and cash accounts at your brokerage. This is a very low risk investment, in the US these accounts are often insured against loss, to a specified limit.

Sometimes an interest bearing investment is *time-locked*. This type of investment requires you to commit your money to be invested for a given period of time for which you receive a set rate of return. Usually, the longer you commit the higher the interest rates. If you withdraw your money before the maturity date, you will usually have to pay an early withdrawal penalty. This is a relatively lower risk investment. Examples are certificates of deposit or some government bonds. Other types of Bonds may have higher yields based on the higher risks from the quality of the issuer's "credit rating".

- *Stocks and Mutual Funds*

This is an investment you make in a company, in which you effectively become a part owner. There is usually no time lock on publicly traded stock, however there may be changes in the tax rates you pay on capital gains depending on how long you hold the stock. Thus, stocks are typically quite liquid, you can access your money relatively quickly. This investment is a higher risk, as you have no guarantee on the future price of a stock.

A mutual fund is a group investment mechanism in which you can buy into many stocks simultaneously. For example, a "S&P 500 index fund" is a fund which purchases all 500 stocks listed in the Standard and Poor's index. When you buy a share of this fund, you are really buying a small amount of each of the 500 stocks contained within the fund. Mutual funds are treated exactly like a single stock, both for tax purposes and in accounting.

- *Fixed Assets*

Assets that increase in value over time are another form of investment. Examples include a house, a plot of land, or a valuable painting. This type of investment is very difficult to determine the value of until you sell it. The tax implications of selling these items is varied, depending on the item. For example, you may have tax relief from selling a house if it is your primary residence, but may would not receive this tax break on an expensive painting.

Fixed asset investments are discussed in Chapter 9, *Capital Gains* and Chapter 18, *Depreciation*. Typically, there is not much to do in terms of accounting for fixed asset investments except recording the buying and selling transactions.

Setting Up Accounts

To setup investment accounts in GnuCash you can either use the predefined investment account hierarchy or create your own. The minimum you need to do to track investments is to setup an asset account for each type of investment you own. However, as we have seen in previous chapters, it is usually more logical to create a structured account hierarchy, grouping related investments together. For example, you may want to group all your publicly traded stocks under a parent account named after the brokerage firm you used to buy the stocks.

Note

Regardless of how you setup your account hierarchy, remember that you can always move accounts around later (without losing the work you've put into them), so your initial account hierarchy does not have to be perfect.

Using Predefined Investment Accounts

The Investment Accounts option of the New Account Hierarchy Setup assistant will automatically create a basic investment account hierarchy for you. To access the predefined investment accounts hierarchy, you must make sure your GnuCash file is open, switch to the Accounts tab, and choose Actions → New Account Hierarchy. This will run the New Account Hierarchy Setup assistant and allow you to select additional accounts to add to your account hierarchy. Choose the Investment Accounts option (along with any others you are interested in). Assuming only investment accounts were selected, this will create an account hierarchy as shown below.

Tip

You can also run the New Account Hierarchy Setup assistant by creating a new GnuCash file.

This is an screen image of the Accounts tab after creating a new file and selecting only the default investment accounts.

You will probably at least want to add a *Bank* account to the Assets and probably an *Equity:Opening Balances* account, as we have done in previous chapters. Don't forget to save your new account file with a relevant name!

Creating Investment Accounts Manually

If you want to set up your own investment accounts hierarchy, you may of course do so. Investments usually have a number of associated accounts that need to be created: an asset account to track the investment itself; an income account to track dividend transactions; and expense accounts to track investment fees and commissions.

Custom Accounts Example

The following is a somewhat more complicated example of setting up GnuCash to track your investments, which has the advantage that it groups each different investment under the brokerage that deals with the investments. This way it is easier to compare the statements you get from your brokerage with the accounts you have in GnuCash and spot where GnuCash differs from the statement.

```
Assets
  Investments
    Brokerage Accounts
      I*Trade
        Stocks
          ACME Corp
        Money Market Funds
          I*Trade Municipal Fund
        Cash
      My Stockbroker
        Money Market Funds
          Active Assets Fund
        Government Securities
          Treas Bond xxx
          Treas Note yyy
        Mutual Funds
          Fund A
          Fund B
        Cash
Income
  Investments
    Brokerage Accounts
      Capital Gains
        I*Trade
        My Stockbroker
      Dividends
        I*Trade
          Taxable
          Non-taxable
        My Stockbroker
          Taxable
          Non-taxable
      Interest Income
        I*Trade
          Taxable
          Non-taxable
        My Stockbroker
          Taxable
```

```
        Non-taxable
Expenses
  Investment Expenses
    Commissions
      I*Trade
      My Stockbroker
    Management Fees
      I*Trade
      My Stockbroker
```

Tip

There really is no standard way to set up your investment account hierarchy. Play around, try different layouts until you find something which divides your investment accounts into logical groups which make sense to you.

Interest Bearing Accounts

Investments which have a fixed or variable rate of interest are one of the simplest and most common form of investments available. Interest bearing investments include your bank account, a certificate of deposit, or any other kind of investment in which you receive interest from the principal. This section will describe how to handle these kinds of investments in GnuCash.

Account Setup

When you purchase the interest bearing investment, you must create an asset account to record the purchase of the investment, an income account to record earnings from interest, and an expense account to record bank charges. Below is an account layout example, in which you have an interest bearing savings account and a certificate of deposit at your bank.

```
Assets
  Bank ABC
    CD
    Savings
Expenses
  Bank ABC
    Charges
Income
  Interest Income
    CD
    Savings
```

As usual, this account hierarchy is simply presented as an example, you should create your accounts in a form which best matches your actual situation.

Example

Now let's populate these accounts with real numbers. Let's assume that you start with $10000 in your bank account, which pays 1% interest and you buy a $5000 certificate of deposit with a 6 month maturity date and a 2% yield. Clearly, it is much better to keep your money in the CD than in the savings account. After the initial purchase, your accounts should look something like this:

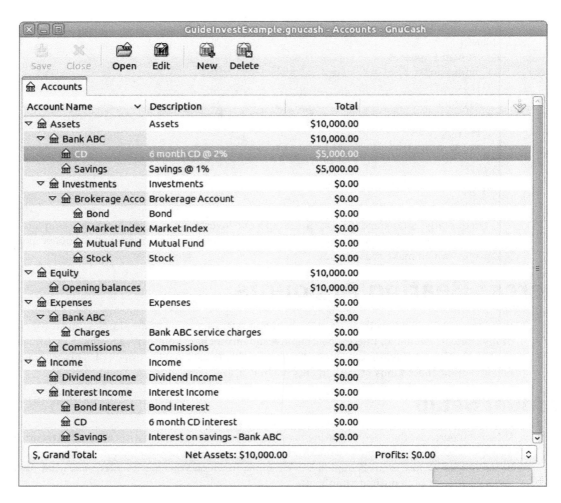

This is an image of the account register after the creation and investing in a CD investment.

Now, during the course of the next 6 month, you receive monthly bank statements which describe the activity of your account. In our fictional example, we do nothing with the money at this bank, so the only activity is income from interest and bank charges. The monthly bank charges are $2. After 6 months, the register window for the CD and for the savings account should look like these:

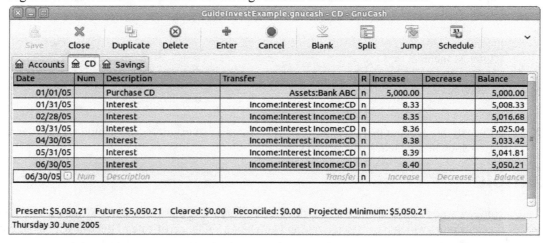

This is an image of the register of the CD account after 6 months.

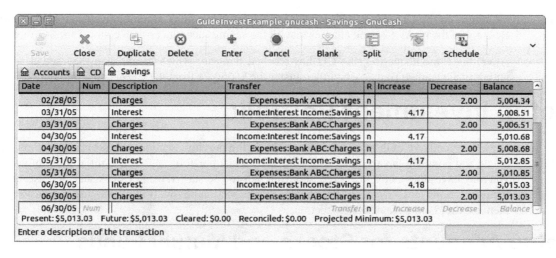

This is an image of the register of the Savings account after 6 months.

And this is the main GnuCash account window:

This a screen capture of the accounts after 6 months.

From the above image of the main GnuCash account window you see a nice summary of what happened to these investments over the 6 months. While the yield on the CD is double that of the savings account, the return on the CD was $50.21 versus $13.03 for the savings account, or almost 4 times more. Why? Because of the pesky $2 bank charges that hit the savings account (which counted for $12 over 6 months).

After this 6 month period, the CD has reached maturity which means you may sell it with no early withdrawal penalty. To do so, simply transfer the $5050.21 from the CD account into the savings account.

Setup Investment Portfolio

Now that you have built an account hierarchy in the previous section, this section will show you how to create and populate the accounts with your investment portfolio. After this initial setup of your portfolio, you may have shares of stock purchased from before you started using GnuCash. For these stocks, follow the instructions in the *Entering Preexisting Shares* section below. If you have just purchased your stocks, then use the *Buying New Shares* section.

Setup Accounts for Stocks and Mutual Funds

This section will show you how to add stocks and mutual fund accounts to GnuCash. In this section, we will assume you are using the basic account setup introduced in the previous section, but the principles can be applied to any account hierarchy.

You should have within the top level Asset account, a few levels down, an account entitled Stock. Open the account tree to this level by clicking on the "right facing triangle marker" signs next to the account names until the tree is opened to the depth of the new account. You will need to create a sub-account (of type *stock*) under the Stock account for every stock you own. Every stock is a separate account. The naming of these stock accounts is usually done using the stock ticker abbreviation, though account names may be anything that is clear to you and other users. So, for example, you could name your accounts *AMZN*, *IBM* and *NST* for your Amazon, IBM and NSTAR stocks respectively. Below is a schematic model of the layout (only showing the Assets sub-accounts).

```
Assets
  Investments
    Brokerage Accounts
      Bond
      Mutual Funds
      Market Index
      Stock
        AMZN
        IBM
        NST
```

Note

If you want to track income (dividends/interest/capital gains) on a per-stock or fund basis, you will need to create an *Income:Dividends:STOCKSYMBOL*, *Income:Cap Gain (Long):STOCKSYMBOL*, *Income:Cap Gain (Short):STOCKSYMBOL* and *Income:Interest:STOCKSYMBOL* account for each stock you own that pays dividends or interest.

Example Stock Account

As an example, let's assume that you currently own 100 shares of Amazon stock. First, create the stock account AMZN by selecting the Stock account and click on the menu Actions+New Account.... The New Account dialog will appear, follow the steps, in the sequence below to setup your new stock account.

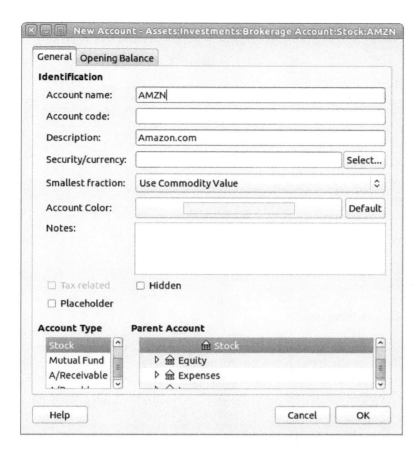

New Account Window

1. *Account Name* - Usually, use the stock ticker abbreviation, IE: "AMZN"

2. *Account Code* - Optional field, use CUSIP, the newspaper listing symbol, mutual fund family ID or code of your own choosing.

3. *Description* - Optional field for detailed description of the commodity/stock. Note this field by default is displayed in the Account tab tree.

4. *Account Type* - Select the type of account you are creating from the lower left-hand list.

5. *Parent Account* - Select the parent account for the new account from the right hand listing. Expand list of accounts if necessary.

6. *Create the New Security* - To use a new stock, you must create the stock as a new commodity

   • *Select Security/Currency* - Click on the Select ... button next to the security/currency line. We must change the security from the default (your default currency) to this specific stock. This will bring up the Select Security dialog.

   • *Type* - Change the type from current to the exchange where the security/commodity is traded (in this example NASDAQ).

   Select the New button to open the New Security window.

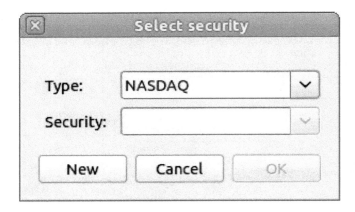

Select Security Window

- *Create the Security* - Click on the New... button and enter the appropriate information for this stock on the new form New Security.

  - The Full name: is "Amazon.com".

  - The Symbol/abbreviation: is "AMZN". The symbol is the stock ticket used in your quote source several lines down on the form. Note that different symbols will be utilized on different price sources for the same stock, an example is Ericsson on the Stockholm Exchange is ERIC-B while on Yahoo it is ERRICB.ST

  - The Type: should already be NASDAQ, because this is what was selected in the security selector, but you can change it here, including adding more categories. More information about this can be found in the Help Manual in section 7.7, "Security Editor".

  - The ISIN, CUSIP or other code is where you can enter some other coding number or text (leave it blank in this example).

  - The Fraction traded should be adjusted to the smallest fraction of this security which can be traded, usually 1/100 or 1/10000.

  - The checkbox "Get Online Quotes", the quote source and the timezone should be selected to define the sources for updating prices on-line. See Also "Setting Stock Price Automatically".

    ### Note

    If the Get Online Quotes button is not highlighted, and it is not tickable, then the Finance::Quote package is not installed. See the section on "Installing Finance::Quote".

    Below is what this window should look like when finished:

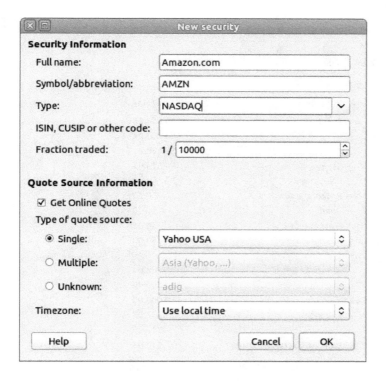

New Security Window

- *Save Security* - Click on the OK button to save this new security, this will close the New Security window and return to the New Account window.

7. *Select the Security* - you should now see the newly created security available in the pull down menu for Security/Currency. Select it (it is probably already selected) and click on OK.

8. *Smallest Fraction* - Specify the smallest fraction of the security/commodity that is traded.

9. *Notes* - Enter any notes or messages related to this security/commodity.

10. *Tax Related* - Go to Edit → Tax Report Options to check this box if this account's transactions will relate to Income Taxes.

11. *Placeholder* - Check box if this account is a "Placeholder", that is it will contain no transactions.

12. *Finished* - You should now have been automatically returned to the New Account dialog, with the symbol/abbreviation: line set to "AMZN (Amazon.com)". Click on OK to save this new stock account.

You have now created the Amazon stock account, your main account should look something like this (notice that there are a few extra accounts here, a bank account, and an equity account):

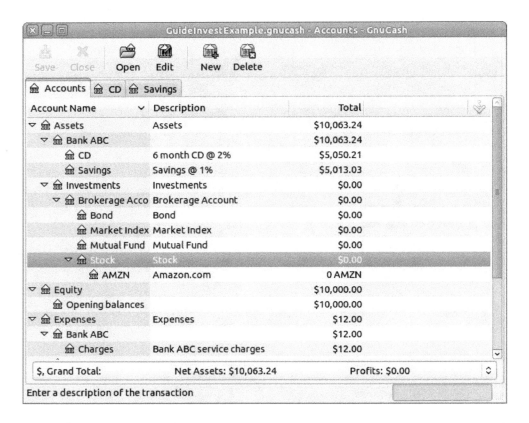

This image is after the creation of the first stock account (AMZN)

Open the account register window for this AMZN stock account (double click on it). Here you see the **Commodity** view. This gives you an overview of the transactions in this commodity including the number of units (shares for a stock or mutual fund) bought or sold, the net price per unit, and the total amount. Obviously, we have not bought or sold any shares of AMZN yet, so the register should not contain any transactions.

Buying Shares

Entering Preexisting Shares

To register the initial 100 shares of this stock that you purchased previously, on the first transaction line, enter the date of the purchase (eg: Jan. 1 2005), a description (eg: Initial Purchase), transfer from *Equity:Opening Balances*, Shares (eg: 100), and Price (eg: $20). You do not need to fill in the Buy column, as it will be calculated for you. This example assumed there was no commission on this transaction to simplify the example. Your AMZN Commodity view should now appear like this:

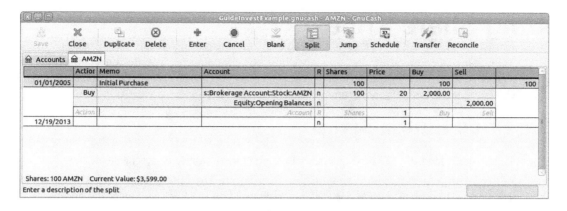

This image is of the transaction register of the AMZN account after the first stock account "purchase".

Notice that the Balance is in the units of the commodity (AMZN shares) not in currency units. Thus, the balance is 100 (AMZN units) rather than $2000. This is how it should be.

Buying New Shares

The only difference between setting up a new stock purchase versus the setup for preexisting stocks as described in the previous section is that instead of transferring the money used to purchase the stock from the *Equity:Opening Balances* account, you use your *Assets:Bank ABC* account.

Now you will purchase $5000 of IBM stock, with a commission of $100. First step will be to create the stock account for IBM. The existing *Expenses:Commissions* account will be used. If you wish to track commissions to the individual stock an additional sub-account would be necessary.

Now for the transaction, on the first transaction line, enter the date of the purchase (eg: Jan. 3 2005), a description (eg: Initial IBM Purchase), Shares will be skipped (to be calculated), Price (eg: $96.60), and Buy ($5000). You do not need to fill in the Shares column, as it will be calculated for you. The next line in the split transaction will be *Expenses:Commissions* and fill in Buy ($100). The third line will be to transfer from *Assets:Bank ABC:Savings*, $5100 to balance the transaction. Your IBM Commodity view should now appear like this:

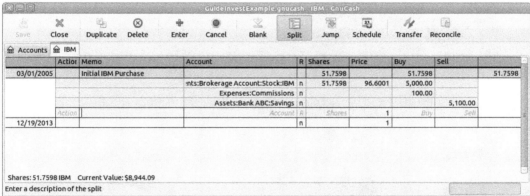

This image is of the transaction register of the IBM account after the first stock account "purchase" with a commission.

Setting Share Price

The value of a commodity, such as a stock, must be explicitly set. The stock accounts track the quantity of stocks you own, but the value of the stock is stored in the *Price Editor*. The values set in the Price Editor can be updated manually or automatically.

Initial Price Editor Setup

To use the Price Editor to track a stock value, you must initially insert the stock. To do so, open the Price Editor (Tools → Price Editor) and click on Add button. The first time a Commodity/Stock is entered this window will be blank except for the control buttons on the bottom. Select the appropriate Commodity you want to insert into the Price Editor. At this point, you can input the price of the commodity manually. There are 6 fields in the New Commodity window:

Namespace	The exchange market where the security/commodity is traded (in this example NASDAQ)
Security	The name of the commodity, must be chosen from the Select... list
Currency	The currency in which the Price is expressed.
Date	Date that the price is valid
Type	One of: Bid (the market buying price), Ask (the market selling price), Last (the last transaction price), Net Asset Value (mutual fund price per share), or Unknown. Stocks and currencies will usually give their quotes as one of bid, ask or last. Mutual funds are often given as net asset value. For other commodities, simply choose Unknown. This option is for informational purposes only, it is not used by GnuCash.
Price	The price of one unit of this commodity.

As an example of adding the AMZN commodity to the price editor, with an initial value of $40.50 per share.

Adding the AMZN commodity to the price editor, with an initial value of $40.50 per share.

Click OK when finished. Once you have performed this initial placement of the commodity into the Price Editor, you will not have to do it again, even if you use the same commodity in another account.

Note

If you have online retrieval of quotes activated (see the section called "Configuring for Automatic Retrieval of Quotes"), you can initialize a commodity without manually making an entry. When you initially add the security in the Security Editor, check Get Online Quotes and save the security. Then, in the Price Editor, click Get Quotes, and the new security will be inserted into the price list with the retrieved price.

Setting Stock Price Manually

If the value of the commodity (stock) changes, you can adjust the value by entering the Price Editor, selecting the commodity, clicking on Edit and entering the new price.

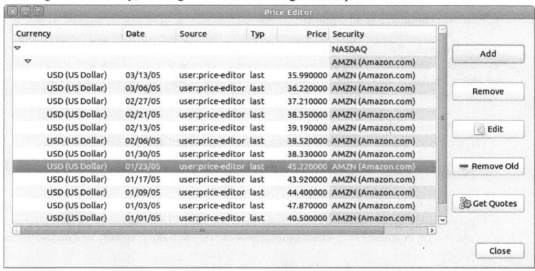

The main price editor window, showing the list of all known commodities.

Configuring for Automatic Retrieval of Quotes

If you have more than a couple of commodities, you will tire of having to update their prices constantly. GnuCash has the ability to automatically download the most recent price for your commodities using the Internet. This is accomplished through the Perl module Finance::Quote, which must be installed in order to activate this feature.

To determine if the Perl module Finance::Quote is already installed on your system, type **perldoc Finance::Quote** in a terminal window and check to see if there is any documentation available. If you see the documentation, then the module is installed, if you do not see the documentation, then it has not been installed.

Installing Finance::Quote

Microsoft Windows:

• Close GnuCash.

- You need to have installed ActivePerl [http://www.activestate.com/store/activeperl]

- Run **Install Online Price Retrieval** in the GnuCash "Start" menu entry.

Mac OS X: You need to have XCode installed. XCode is an optional item from your OS X distribution DVD. Run the **Update Finance Quote** app in the GnuCash dmg. You can run it from the dmg or copy it to the same folder to which you copied GnuCash. It will open a Terminal window and run a script for you which will ask lots of questions. Accept the default for each unless you know what you're doing.

Linux:

- Close any running GnuCash instances.

- Locate the folder where GnuCash is installed by searching for gnc-fq-update

- Change to that directory, open a root shell

- Run the command **gnc-fq-update**

This will launch a Perl CPAN update session that will go out onto the internet and install the Finance::Quote module on your system. The gnc-fq-update program is interactive, however, with most systems you should be able to answer "no" to the first question: "Are you ready for manual configuration? [yes]" and the update will continue automatically from that point.

After installation is complete, you should run the "gnc-fq-dump" test program, in the same directory, distributed with GnuCash to test if Finance::Quote is installed and working properly.

Note

If you feel uncomfortable about performing any of these steps, please either email the GnuCash-user mailing list (<gnucash-user@gnucash.org>) for help or come to the GnuCash IRC channel on irc.gnome.org. You can also leave out this step and manually update your stock prices.

Configuring Securities for Online Quotes

With Finance::Quote installed and functioning correctly, you must configure your GnuCash securities to use this feature to obtain updated price information automatically. Whether creating new securities or modifying securities that have already been setup, use the Tools → Security Editor, to edit the security and check the Get Online Quotes box. You will now be able to modify the radio buttons for Type of quote source, the pull-down menus to specify the specific source(s) and The timezone for these quotes. When finished editing, Close the Security Editor to return to the Price Editor and click on the Get Quotes button to update your stock prices on the Internet.

The command **gnucash --add-price-quotes $HOME/gnucash-filename** can be used to fetch the current prices of your stocks. The file specified $HOME/gnucash-filename will depend on the name and location of your data file. This can be determined by the name displayed in the top frame of the GnuCash window, before the "-". The file name can also be found under File in the recently opened file list; the first item, numbered 1, is the name of the currently open file.

This can be automated by creating a crontab entry. For example, to update your file every Friday evening (16:00) after the relevant exchange markets close (modify the time accordingly for your time zone), you could add the following to your personal crontab:

0 16 * * 5 gnucash --add-price-quotes $HOME/gnucash-filename > /dev/null 2>&1

Remember that Mutual Fund "prices" are really "Net Asset Value" and require several hours after the exchange closes before being available. If NAVs are downloaded before the current days NAVs are determined, yesterday's NAVs are retrieved.

Displaying Share Value

The main account window, by default, only shows the quantity of each commodity that you own, under the column heading Total. In the case of stocks, this commodity is the number of shares. Often, however, you will want to see the value of your stocks expressed in terms of some monetary unit. This is easily accomplished by entering the main window, selecting the Accounts tab, by clicking on the *Titlebar* Options button (the small down pointing arrow on the right side of the main account window titles bar), and selecting the option to display the account total field "Total (USD)". You will see a new column in the main window entitled Total (USD) that will express the value of all commodities in the report currency.

Viewing the value of a stock commodity in the main window using the Total in Report Currency option.

Selecting "Price Source" in Stock Value Reports

Most GnuCash Asset reports have options to set/modify a number of parameters for the report. The Options windows is displayed by selecting the report tab then clicking on either the Options icon in the *Menubar* or selecting Edit → Report Options. The General tab in the resulting window contains various parameters for the report. One of these is "Price Source" which of offers three alternatives to determine stock prices in reports:

Note

In the example below, the report is a customization of the **Average Balance** report in the Assets & Liabilities reports submenu.

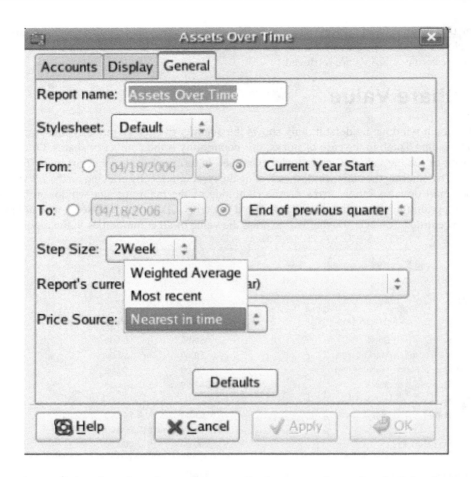

Determining the value of a stock commodity in a report by setting the Price Source option.

- Weighted Average - gives you a graph of the weighted price of all *transactions*. It will *not* take into account prices defined in the price editor.

- Most recent - displays the changing value of your stocks based solely on *the most recent* price available from the price editor. The price figuring in your stock transactions is *not* considered.

- Nearest in time - the graph is exclusively based on the prices available from the price editor. The value of your stock at each step and point in time is calculated based on the nearest available price in the price editor.

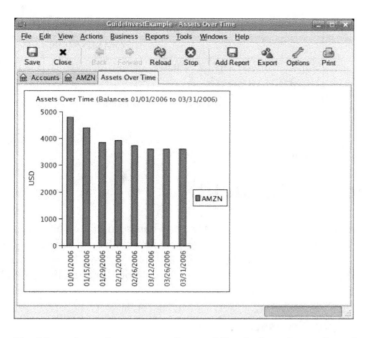

Tracking what value your stocks would've had on the stock exchanges.

Selling Shares

Entering an investment you are selling is done in the same way as buying one (see the section called "Buying New Shares") except the total cost of the transaction is entered in the *Sell* column and the *Shares* column is entered as a negative amount. The net proceeds from the sale should be transferred from the stock account to your bank or brokerage account.

The proper recording of the stock sale *must* be done using a split transaction. In the split transaction, you must account for the profit (or loss) as coming from an *Income:Capital Gains* account (or *Expenses:Capital Loss*). To balance this income, you will need to enter the stock asset twice in the split. Once to record the actual sale (using the correct number of shares and correct price per share) and once to balance the income profit (setting the number of shares to 0 and price per share to 0).

Note

In order to get GnuCash to commit this zero-share, zero-price split to the transaction, you *must* **Tab** out of the split. If you use the **Enter** key, GnuCash will convert the split into shares of the commodity.

In the split transaction scheme presented below, the symbol NUM_SHARES is the number of shares you are selling, SELL_PRICE is the price for which you sold the shares, GROSS_SALE is the total price for which you sold shares, equal to NUM_SHARES*SELL_PRICE. PROFIT is the amount of money you made on the sale. COMMISSIONS are the brokerage commissions. NET_SALE is the net amount of money received from the sale, equal to GROSS_SALE - COMMISSIONS.

Table 8.1. Selling Stock using Split Transaction Scheme

Account	Number of Shares	Share Price	Total Buy	Total Sell
Assets:Bank ABC			NET_SALE	

Assets:Stock:SYMBOL	0	0	PROFIT	(Loss)
Expenses:Commissions			COMMISSION	
Assets:Stock:SYMBOL	-NUM_SHARES	SELL_PRICE		GROSS_SALE
Income:Capital Gains			(Loss)	PROFIT

If you will be recording the sale of the stock as a capital gain (or loss), please see Chapter 9, *Capital Gains* and Chapter 18, *Depreciation* for more information on this topic.

Example - Sale of stock with profit

As an example we will use the AMZN account created in the previous section. So you bought 100 shares of AMZN for $20 per share, then later sell them all for $36 per share with a commission of $75. In the split transaction scheme above, PRICEBUY is $20 (the original buying price), NUM_SHARES is 100, TOTALBUY is $2000 (the original buying cost), GROSS_SALE is $3600, and finally PROFIT is $1525 (GROSS_SALE-TOTALBUY-COMMISSION).

Table 8.2. Selling Stock Split Transaction Scheme

Account	Shares	Price	Buy	Sell
Assets:Bank ABC			3525.00	
Assets:Brokerage Account:Stock:AMZN	0	0	1600.00	
Expenses:Commissions			75.00	
Assets:Brokerage Account:Stock:AMZN	-100	36.00		3600.00
Income:Cap Gain (Long):AMZN				1600.00

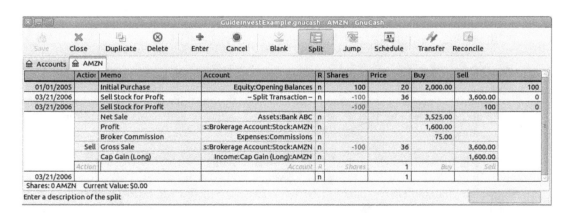

An example of selling stock for gain. You bought 100 shares of AMZN for $20 per share, and sold for $36.

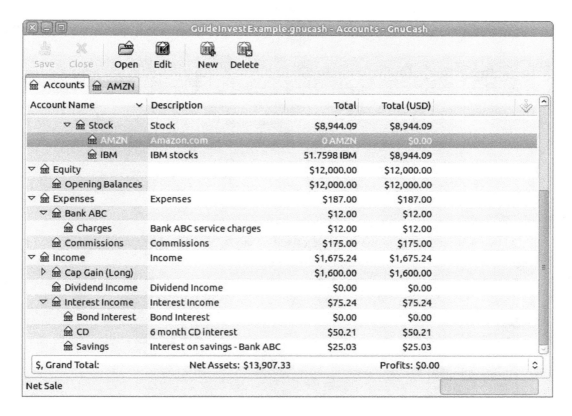

An image of the account tree after the example of selling stock for gain.

Example - Sale of stock with loss

As an example we will use the IBM account created in the previous section. You then have bought 51.7598 shares of IBM for $96.6001 per share, then later sell them all for $90 per share. In the split transaction scheme below, PRICEBUY is $96.6001 (the original buying price), NUM_SHARES is 51.7598, TOTAL_BUY is $5,000 (the original buying price), (Loss) is $341.62, and finally GROSS_SALE is $4658.38. Assume the commission was $100.00.

Table 8.3. Selling Shares at loss Split Transaction Scheme

Account	Shares	Price	Buy	Sell
Assets:Bank ABC			4558.38	
Assets:Brokerage Account:Stock:IBM	0	0		341.62
Expenses:Commissions			100	
Assets:Brokerage Account:Stock:IBM	-51.7598	90.00		4658.38
Income:Cap Gain (Long):IBM			341.62	0

Note

You may either enter the loss as a positive number in the "buy" column or as a negative number in the "sell" column, GnuCash will move the "negative profit" to the other column.

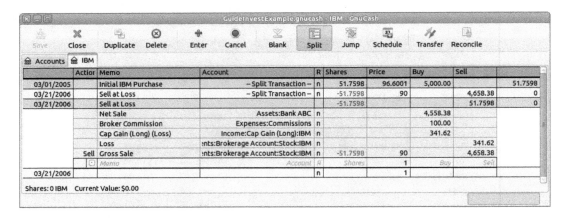

Above is a screenshot of the example of selling stock. You bought $5000 worth of IBM shares with a stock value of $96.6001, and sold for $90.

An image of the account tree after the example of selling stock for loss.

Dividends

Some companies or mutual funds pay periodic dividends to shareholders. Dividends are typically given in one of two ways, either they are automatically reinvested into the commodity or they are given as cash. Mutual funds are often setup to automatically reinvest the dividend, while common stock dividends usually pay cash.

Dividends in Cash

If the dividend is presented as cash, you should record the transaction in the asset account that received the money, as income from *Income:Dividends*. Additionally if you want to tie the cash dividend to a particular stock holding then add a dummy transaction split to the stock account with quantity 0 price 1 value 0.

As an example consider the following; the dividends deposited as cash into the *Broker* Account with a tie to the stock account.

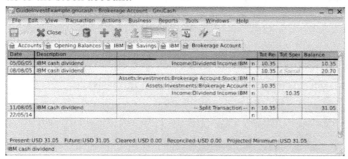

An image of the *Brokerage* Account register after a series of cash dividends.

Note

If you want to track dividends on a per-stock basis, you would need to create an *Income:Dividends:STOCKSYMBOL* account for each stock you own that pays dividends.

Dividends Re-Invested

If you receive the dividend in the form of an automatic reinvestment, the transaction for this should be handled within the stock or mutual fund account as income from "Income:Dividend" for the appropriate number of reinvested shares. This type of reinvest account is often referred to as a DRIP (Dividend Re-Investment Program).

As an example consider the following purchase of NSTAR (NST) stock with the dividends reinvested into a DRIP Account. Mutual fund re-investments would be the same.

Starting with the purchase of 100 shares on Jan. 3, 2005, all dividends will be reinvested and an account is created to track the dividend to the specific stock. GnuCash simplifies the entry by allowing calculations within the cells of the transaction. If the first dividend is $.29/share, enter $53.28 (purchase price + dividend) in the share Price cell and 100*.29 in the Buy cell. GnuCash will calculate for you the corresponding numer of Shares

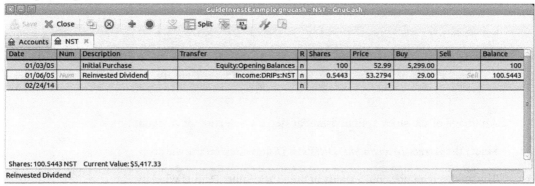

An image of the NST Stock Account register after a dividend reinvestment.

Splits and Mergers

Companies may split their stock for many reasons but the most common is that the price has risen higher than management thinks is a reasonable price for many investors. Some of these splits are simple exchanges (eg 2 for 1 or 3 for 2) and some are complex exchanges with cash distributions. Splits may also result in fewer shares if the exchange rate is a reverse split (1 for 3 or .75 for 1).

Simple Stock Split

As an example, our holding of NST stock declared a 2 for 1 stock split effective June 6, 2005. The process for entering this transaction is; select Actions → Stock Split to start the assistant.

An image of the selection of the stock split assistant.

The first screen is an Introduction, select Forward to display the selection of the account and stock for the split. You will need to create an entry for each *Account:Stock* combination you hold.

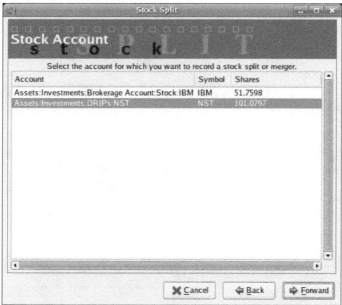

An image of the stock split assistant at step 2 - Selection of Account/Stock.

Select the *Assets:Investments:DRIPs:NST* and click on Forward.

The next screen presents 5 fields in the Stock Splits Details window:

- Date - Enter the date of the split.

- Shares - The number of shares increased (or decreased) in the transaction.

  In our example it is a 2 for 1 split so the number of additional shares is the number of shares currently in the register.

- Description - The Description should give a brief explanation of the transaction.

- New Price - If desired the new price of the stock, after the split, may be entered.

- Currency - The currency of the transaction is required. This should be the same as the stock purchase currency.

Click on the Forward button.

An image of the stock split assistant at step 3 - Split Details.

The next screen will be skipped in this example as there was no "Cash in Lieu".

An image of the stock split assistant at step 4 - Cash in Lieu.

A final Finish screen will give a last option to; Cancel, Back to modify any data entered or Apply to complete the stock split with the data entered.

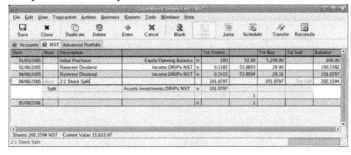

An image of the *Assets:Investments:DRIPs:NST* register after a simple stock split transaction.

Moderately Complex Stock Merger

As an example, assume you held AT&T stock during the Nov. 18, 2005 merger of SBC with AT&T. For this example you will have purchased AT&T on April 1, 2005, any dividends will have been paid in cash, therefore not entered into the AT&T stock register.

The conditions of the merger were .77942 share of SBC stock were exchanged for each share of AT&T stock. The merged company continued to use the symbol "T" from AT&T.

AT&T paid a "dividend" of $1.20/share on the transaction date, however this will not appear in the stock account as it was a cash distribution.

The process for entering this transaction is identical to the simple split until the "Details" screen. You will need to create an split entry in each *Investment Account:Stock* account combination that has shares splitting.

An image of the stock split assistant at step 2 - Selection of Account/Stock (*Investment Account:T*).

Select the *Assets:Investments:Brokerage Account:Stock:T* and click on Forward.

The next screen presents 5 fields in the Stock Splits Details window:

• Date - Enter the date of the split. Here we'll enter November 18, 2005.

• Shares - The number of shares increased (or decreased) in the transaction.

In our example it is a .77942 for 1 split so the number of shares will decrease from the number of shares currently in the register. You may use GnuCash's ability to preform calculations on an entry form by entering data directly (E.g. "(.77942*100)-100") to calculate the decrease in shares from the split.

• Description - The Description should give a brief explanation of the transaction.

• New Price - If desired the new price of the stock, after the split, may be entered.

• Currency - The currency of the transaction is required. This should be the same as the stock purchase currency.

Click on the Forward button.

An image of the stock split assistant at step 3 - Split Details.

The next screen will be skipped in this example as there was no "Cash in Lieu".

A final "Finish" screen will give a last option to Back to modify any data entered or Apply to complete the stock split with the data entered.

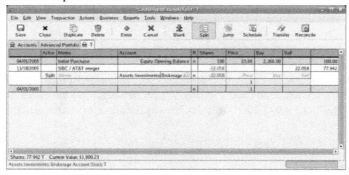

An image of the *Investment Account:T* register after a stock split transaction that decreases the shares.

Chapter 9. Capital Gains

This chapter will present some of the techniques used to keep track of the unrealized and realized gains and losses, better known as capital gains and losses.

Basic Concepts

This chapter will present some of the techniques used to keep track of the unrealized and realized gains and losses, better known as capital gains and losses.

Certain resellable assets can change value over time, such as stocks, bonds, houses, or cars. Some assets (eg: a stock) could increase in value, some (eg: a car) could decrease in value. It is important to be able to track some of these time-dependent asset valuations, this chapter will show you how.

Probably everything you own will increase or decrease in value over time. So, the question is for which of these assets should you track this changing value? The simple answer is that you only need to track this for items which could be sold for cash in the future or which relate to taxation.

Consumable and disposable items (eg: food, gas for your car, or printer paper) are obviously not involved. Thus, even though the new clothes you recently bought will certainly depreciate, you would not want to track this depreciation since you have no intention of reselling the clothes and there is no tax implications to the depreciation on clothing. So, for this example, the purchase of new clothes should be recorded as a pure expense... you spent the money, and it is gone.

Asset appreciation occurs when something you own increases in value over time. When you own an asset which has increased in value, the difference between the original purchase price and the new value is known as *unrealized gains*. When you sell the asset, the profit you earn is known as *realized gains* or *capital gains*. An example of an asset from which you could have unrealized gains, and eventually capital gains, is stock in a publicly traded company.

Estimating Valuation

As mentioned in the introduction to this chapter, capital gains are the profits received from the sale of an asset. This section will describe how to record capital gains in GnuCash.

The accounting methods for handling asset appreciation differs somewhat from depreciation because typically you are only concerned with the moment you sell the asset and realize the capital gains. This is opposed to the continuous nature of tracking depreciation. Capital gains are an important subject in the world of taxation, because governments tend to be quite interested in taxing capital gains in one manner or another.

Note

As always, there are exceptions. If you hold a bond that pays all of its interest at maturity, tax authorities often require that you recognize interest each year, and refuse this to be treated as a capital gain. Consult the appropriate tax codes to determine the preferred treatment for each type of asset you have which may be affected by capital gains taxes.

Estimating the increasing value of assets is generally not simple, because often it is difficult to know its exact value until the moment it is sold.

Securities traded daily on open markets such as stock exchanges are possibly the easiest type of asset to predict the value of, and selling the asset at market prices may be as simple as calling a broker and issuing a Market Order. On the other hand, estimating the value of a house is more difficult. Homes are sold less often than stocks, and the sales tend to involve expending considerable effort and negotiations, which means that estimates are likely to be less precise. Similarly, selling a used automobile involves a negotiation process that makes pricing a bit less predictable.

Values of collectible objects such as jewelry, works of art, baseball cards, and "Beanie Babies" are even harder to estimate. The markets for such objects are much less open than the securities markets and less open than the housing market. Worse still are one-of-a-kind assets. Factories often contain presses and dies customized to build a very specific product that cost tens or hundreds of thousands of dollars; this equipment may be worthless outside of that very specific context. In such cases, several conflicting values might be attached to the asset, none of them unambiguously correct.

The general rule of thumb in accounting for estimating unrealized gains (or loses) is that you should only revalue assets such as stocks which are readily sellable and for which there are very good estimates of the value. For all other assets, it is better to simply wait until you sell them, at which time you can exactly determine the capital gains. Of course, there is no hard rule on this, and in fact different accountants may prefer to do this differently.

Account Setup

As with most accounting practices, there are a number of different ways to setup capital gains accounts. We will present here a general method which should be flexible enough to handle most situations. The first account you will need is an *Asset Cost* account (GnuCash account type Asset), which is simply a place where you record the original purchase of the asset. Usually this purchase is accomplished by a transaction from your bank account.

In order to keep track of the appreciation of the asset, you will need three accounts. The first is an *Unrealized Gains* asset account in which to collect the sum of all of the appreciation amounts. The *Unrealized Gains* asset account is balanced by a *Unrealized Gains* income account, in which all periodic appreciation income is recorded. Finally, another income account is necessary, called a *Realized Gains* in which you record the actual capital gains upon selling the asset.

Below is a generic account hierarchy for tracking the appreciation of 2 assets, *ITEM1* and *ITEM2*. The *Assets:Fixed Assets:ITEM1:Cost* accounts are balanced by the *Assets:Current Assets:Savings Account* account, the *Assets:Fixed Assets:ITEM1:Unrealized Gains* accounts are balanced by the *Income:Unrealized Gains* account (similar for *ITEM2*).

```
-Assets
  -Current Assets
    -Savings Account
  -Fixed Assets
    -ITEM1
      -Cost
      -Unrealized Gain
    -ITEM2
      -Cost
      -Unrealized Gain
-Income
  -Realized Gains
  -Unrealized Gains
```

Example

Let's suppose you buy an asset expected to increase in value, say a Degas painting, and want to track this. (The insurance company will care about this, even if nobody else does.)

Start with an account hierarchy similar to that shown in the section called "Account Setup", but replace "ITEM1" with "Degas" and you can remove the "ITEM2" accounts. We will assume that the Degas painting had an initial value of one hundred thousand dollars. Begin by giving your self $100,000 in the bank and then transferring that from your bank account to your *Assets:Fixed Assets:Degas:Cost* account (the asset purchase transaction). You should now have a main account window which appears like this:

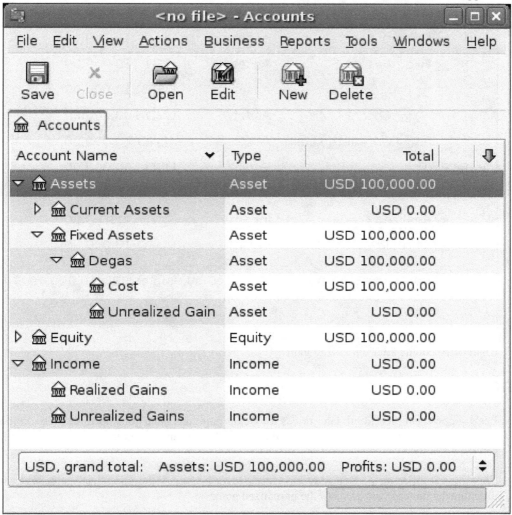

The asset appreciation example main window

Unrealized Gains

A month later, you have reason to suspect that the value of your painting has increased by $10,000 (an unrealized gain). In order to record this you transfer $10,000 from your *Accrued Gains* income account (*Income:Unrealized Gains*) to your asset Unrealized Gains account (*Assets:Fixed Assets:Degas:Unrealized Gain*). Your main window will resemble this:

Chart of Accounts after unrealized gain

Selling

Let's suppose another month later prices for Degas paintings have gone up some more, in this case about $20,000, you estimate. You duly record the $20,000 as an unrealized income like above, then decide to sell the painting.

Three possibilities arise. You may have *accurately estimated* the unrealized gain, *underestimated* the unrealized gain, or *overestimated* the unrealized gain.

1. *Accurate estimation* of unrealized gain.

   Your optimistic estimate of the painting's value was correct. First you must record that the profits made are now realized gains, not unrealized gains. Do this by transferring the income from the *Income:Unrealized Gains* to the *Income:Realized Gains* account.

   Secondly, you must credit your bank account with the selling price of the painting. This money comes directly from your *Assets:Fixed Assets:Degas* sub-accounts. Transfer the full *Assets:Fixed Assets:Degas:Cost* value into *Assets:Current Assets:Savings Account*, and the full *Assets:Fixed Assets:Degas:Unrealized Gain* into *Assets:Current Assets:Savings Account*.

These transactions should now appear as follows:

Table 9.1. Turning an Accrued Gain into a Realized Gain

Account	Transfer to	Transaction Amount	Account Total
Income:Unrealized Gains	Income:Realized Gains	$30,000	$0
Assets:Fixed Assets:Degas:Cost	Assets:Current Assets:Savings Account	$100,000	$0
Assets:Fixed Assets:Degas:Unrealized Gains	Assets:Current Assets:Savings Account	$30,000	$0

This leaves the *Assets:Current Assets:Savings Account* account with a total of $130000 and *Income:Realized Gains* with a total of $30000.

Chart of Accounts after realized gain

2. *Under estimation* of unrealized gain.

You were over-optimistic about the value of the painting. Instead of the $130000 you thought the painting was worth you are only offered $120000. But you still decide to sell, because you value $120000 more than you value the painting. The numbers change a little bit, but not too dramatically.

The transactions should now appear as follows (observe the last transaction which balances the *Unrealized Gains* accounts):

Table 9.2. Turning an Accrued Gain into a Realized Gain

Account	Transfer to	Transaction Amount	Account Total
Income:Unrealized Gains	Income:Realized Gains	$20,000	$10,000
Assets:Fixed Assets:Degas:Cost	Assets:Current Assets:Savings Account	$100,000	$0
Assets:Fixed Assets:Degas:Unrealized Gains	Assets:Current Assets:Savings Account	$20,000	$10,000
Assets:Fixed Assets:Degas:Unrealized Gains	Income:Unrealized Gains	$10,000	$0

This leaves the *Assets:Current Assets:Savings Account* account with a total of $120000 and *Income:Realized Gains* with a total of $20000.

3. *Over estimation* of unrealized gain.

You manage to sell your painting for more than you thought in your wildest dreams ($150,000). The extra value is, again, recorded as a gain, i.e. an income.

The transactions should now appear as follows (observe the last transaction which balances the Unrealized Gains accounts):

Table 9.3. Turning an Accrued Gain into a Realized Gain

Account	Transfer to	Transaction Amount	Account Total
Income:Unrealized Gains	Income:Realized Gains	$50,000	$-20,000
Assets:Fixed Assets:Degas:Cost	Assets:Current Assets:Savings Account	$100,000	$0
Assets:Fixed Assets:Degas:Unrealized Gains	Assets:Current Assets:Savings Account	$50,000	$-20,000
Income:Unrealized Gains	Assets:Fixed Assets:Degas:Unrealized Gains	$20,000	$0

This leaves the *Assets:Current Assets:Savings Account* account with a total of $150,000 and *Income:Realized Gains* with a total of $50,000.

Caution about Valuation

As we see in this example, for non-financial assets, it may be difficult to correctly estimate the "true" value of an asset. It is quite easy to count yourself rich based on questionable estimates that do not reflect "money in the bank".

When dealing with appreciation of assets,

- Be careful with your estimation of values. Do not indulge in wishful thinking.

- Never, ever, count on money you do not have in your bank or as cash. Until you have actually sold your asset and got the money, any numbers on paper (or magnetic patterns on your hard disk) are merely that. If you could realistically convince a banker to lend you money, using the assets as collateral, that is a pretty reasonable evidence that the assets have value, as lenders are professionally suspicious of dubious overestimations of value. Be aware: all too many companies that appear "profitable" on paper go out of business as a result of running out of cash, precisely because "valuable assets" were not the same thing as cash.

Taxation

Taxation policies vary considerably between countries, so it is virtually impossible to say anything that will be universally useful. However, it is common for income generated by capital gains to not be subject to taxation until the date that the asset is actually sold, and sometimes not even then. North American home owners usually find that when they sell personal residences, capital gains that occur are exempt from taxation. It appears that other countries treat sale of homes differently, taxing people on such gains. German authorities, for example, tax those gains only if you owned the property for less than ten years.

Chris Browne has a story from his professional tax preparation days where a family sold a farm, and expected a considerable tax bill that turned out to be virtually nil due to having owned the property before 1971 (wherein lies a critical "Valuation Day" date in Canada) and due to it being a dairy farm, with some really peculiar resulting deductions. The point of this story is that while the presentation here is fairly simple, taxation often gets terribly complicated...

Chapter 10. Multiple Currencies

This chapter will show you how to setup your GnuCash accounts to use multiple currencies.

Basic Concepts

GnuCash supports over a hundred currencies, from the Andorran Franc to the Zimbabwe Dollar. For example, you can have a bank account setup in Euros, and another using Hong Kong Dollars.

Some of the issues which arise when using multiple currencies are, how do you transfer funds between accounts with different currencies? How do you calculate the overall value when you have mixed currency accounts? How do reports deal with mixed currencies?

Note

An alternative way to manage multiple currency accounts from the one presented in the next sections, is to use the trading accounts capabilities of GnuCash. This feature, which has been introduced with GnuCash version 2.3.14, can be enabled by going to the Accounts tab under File → Properties.

For a complete guide on trading accounts you can take a look at this tutorial by Peter Selinger [http://www.mathstat.dal.ca/~selinger/accounting/tutorial.html].

Account Setup

Your default account currency is set in the Account tab under Edit → Preferences (GnuCash → Preferences on Mac OS X). You should set this parameter correctly, as it will save you much time when building your account structure.

Similarly, GnuCash offers an option to set your preferred currency for displaying reports (like the balance sheet and income statement). The option is called Default Report Currency, and is in the Reports tab of the GnuCash Preferences screen. You'll want to set both options when you start using GnuCash because if (for example) your accounts are all in Canadian Dollars but the generated reports are all in US Dollars, the reports will just say that there is "no data/transactions (or only zeroes) for the selected time period".

When you create a new account, you have the option to define the commodity. For currency accounts, you can specify any one of the hundreds of currencies supported by GnuCash by simply selecting it from the currency commodity list. You will notice that the default currency is always whatever you have defined in the preferences. So, if you mostly work with Euros, but have the occasional Ethiopian Birr account, be sure to set your preferences to Euro.

As an example, let's set up a typical bank account scenario where you mostly work in US Dollars, but do also have a European bank account using the Euro currency, as well as one bank account in Hong Kong using Hong Kong Dollars. So, setup 3 bank accounts, one using the Euro currency, one in US Dollars, and another in Hong Kong Dollars. One possible account structure for this would be:

```
-Assets            (USD)
  -Current Assets    (USD)
   -US Bank          (USD)
   -European Bank    (EUR)
   -HK Bank        (HKD)
```

```
-Equity                (USD)
  -Opening Balances
    -USD         (USD)
    -EUR         (EUR)
    -EUR         (HKD)
```

Note: the currency of each account is shown in parenthesis.

Since in this example you mostly work in USD, all of the parent accounts are set to USD. Of course, if you mostly work in Euros, you could change the currency of these parent accounts to EUR. The totals shown in the account tree window will always be converted to the currency of each particular account. Notice, we also set up 3 Starting Balances equity accounts, used to initially populate the 3 banks.

Note

You could also setup just a single Starting Balance account and use a currency transfer to populate the "different currency" accounts. However, this is more advanced option, which is explained in a later section (the section called "Purchase of an asset with foreign currency".

Below you see the result of this example, in which you start with USD 10,000, EUR 10,000 as well as HKD 10,000 in the three bank accounts. Notice that the total of the parent accounts only show the value of the currency of sub-accounts with matching currencies. In the future you can setup the exchange rates between the currencies, and the parent accounts will calculate the converted value of all sub-accounts. See the later section (the section called "Recording/Updating Currency Exchange (How-To)") on how to do this.

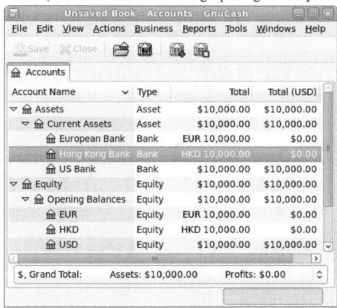

Initial setup of 3 bank accounts with different currencies.

Notice that the "Total (Report)" column is being displayed. This is configured in the column header row, select Arrow down and select "Total(USD)".

User-Defined Currencies

Usually when we talk about currencies, we mean government-backed currencies (or more precisely, currencies defined in the international standard called ISO 4217 [http://en.wikipedia.org/wiki/ISO_4217]).

GnuCash does not allow you to create your own currencies. If you want to track non-ISO currencies, you can use either of two workarounds, depending on which fits your needs better.

Let's say for example that you want to track RewardMiles, which count how many loyalty points you've earned by buying from a certain group of businesses. The account which tracks your RewardMiles will be *Assets:Other:LoyaltyGroupRewardMiles*.

The first method is to define a new security, of type FUND, called RewardMiles. This is pretty straightforward–when you create the new *LoyaltyGroupRewardMiles* account, just set the account type to Stock or Mutual Fund, click the Select... button next to the Security/currency: box, and click New to define a new security of type FUND.

This is not really what the stock and mutual fund account types are meant for, but GnuCash usually lets you decide how you want to use it, instead of dictating. The downside is that you'll have to enter a "price" for every transaction involving RewardMiles, because GnuCash needs the prices to figure out the monetary value of RewardMiles and treat them as one of your assets.

The second method is to use one of the "dummy" currencies to track the RewardMiles. The dummy currencies are "XTS (Code for testing purposes)" and "XXX (No currency)". If you use one of these for your LoyaltyGroupRewardMiles account, you can enter transactions into the account without having to enter share prices for every transaction. And, you can keep using the same two dummy currencies to track all sorts of amounts–vacation dollars earned and used so far this year, vacation hours earned and used, health insurance benefits allowance used and remaining, and so on. You can well imagine that GnuCash can be used as a hub for all sorts of personal metrics, in addition to finances.

The drawback with this second method is that you cannot define exchange rates for the dummy currencies to convert them to ISO currencies. If you want to do that, you really should use the first method.

Recording/Updating Currency Exchange (How-To)

GnuCash allows you to update the Currency Exchange Rates in two different ways, manually and automatically. In the following two sections we will work through both ways.

Before we start, let's have a quick look at the Chart of Accounts

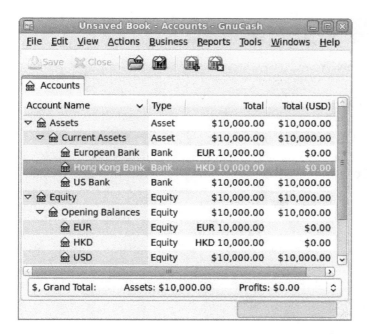

Initial setup of 3 bank accounts with different currencies.

Manually Updating Exchange Rates

Open the Price Editor by going to Tools → Price Editor.

Price Editor Window.

Click on the Add button to add a new currency exchange. A window will appear in which you can setup a new exchange rate. This window should appear like this:

Add Price Editor Window

Set the Namespace to Currency and the Security to EUR (Euro). Then set the exchange rate between the selected security and the selected currency. In this example, you will set the exchange rate to 1 EUR for 1 USD (think of it as: how many units of the currency, in this case, USD, do you have to spend to get one unit of the security, in this case, the currency EUR).

The Price Editor window after setting the exchange rate between Euros and US Dollars

Chart of Accounts after setting the exchange rate between Euros and US Dollars.

Observe that since you have no exchange rate for HKD, GnuCash doesn't convert the HKD accounts to USD. This will be added in the next section.

Automatic Updating Exchange Rates (How-To)

In the previous section you saw how you could manually define a new currency exchange rate, but there must be an easier way to do it. And there is.

Open the Price Editor by going to Tools → Price Editor.

Price Editor Window before you obtain online quotes.

Click on the Get Quotes button to automatically load the various exchange rates you need.

Note

If the Get Quotes button is disabled, that means that the Perl module Finance::Quote is not installed. For information on how to install it, please see the section called "Configuring for Automatic Retrieval of Quotes"

Price Editor Window after we obtained online quotes.

You can observe that GnuCash will download exchange rates for all currencies you are using in your various accounts. This will happen every time you click on Get Quotes or have GnuCash downloading quotes/exchange rates automatically as per the section called "Configuring for Automatic Retrieval of Quotes"

And if you check the main Chart of Accounts you will see that GnuCash has automatically converted the HKD amount to USD amount on the parent accounts that are in USD, as well as on the Total (USD) column. Also the Euro accounts have been been updated with the latest exchange rate.

Chart of Accounts after we obtain online quotes.

Disabling Exchange Rate Retrieval

Whenever you create an account that uses a non-default currency, exchange rate retrieval will be automatically enabled for that currency. However, if you later delete that account, GnuCash will not automatically disable exchange rate retrieval for that currency.

If you have deleted the last account for a particular currency, and you do not wish to retrieve exchange rates for that currency anymore, do the following:

• Open the Securities window by selecting Tools → Security Editor.

• Make sure the Show National Currencies box is selected.

- Expand the CURRENCY row.

- Double click on the currency for which you want to disable exchange rate retrieval.

- Deselect the Get Online Quotes box and click OK.

Recording Purchases in a Foreign Currency (How-To)

You can do it in two different ways.

1) Use GnuCash build in currency exchange between accounts when you do your transactions. This is mainly used for one time transactions, and nothing which happens regularly.

2) Use separate accounts for this Purchase, where all involved accounts use the same currency. This is the recommended method, since it allows much better tracking and follow up. In this way, you do one currency exchange transaction, and after that you do normal transactions.

The rest of this section will explain more based upon option 2).

Purchase of an asset with foreign currency

Your normal place of residence is in Florida, therefore you are using USD as your default currency. But, you do like to travel to the Bahamas and go fishing. You like it so much that you decided to purchase a boat there. To do this, you opened a bank account in Jamaica, moved some money from the US, and then purchased your dream boat (smallest version).

To record this in GnuCash we use the following basic account structure:

```
-Assets                (USD)
  -Current Assets      (USD)
    -US Bank           (USD)
    -Jamaican Bank     (JMD)
  -Fixed Assets        (USD)
    -Boat          (JMD)
-Equity                (USD)
  -Opening Balances
    -USD         (USD)
```

Note: the currency of each account is shown in parenthesis.

First you need to transfer some money ($10,000) to Jamaica, and you use your normal US bank account (with a balance of $100,000) for that. The bank gives you an exchange rate of USD 1 = JMD 64, but charges you USD 150 to transfer the money.

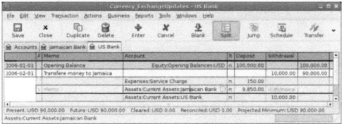

Transfer money to Jamaica

Select the Jamaica transaction line ($9,850.00), right click and select Edit Exchange Rate

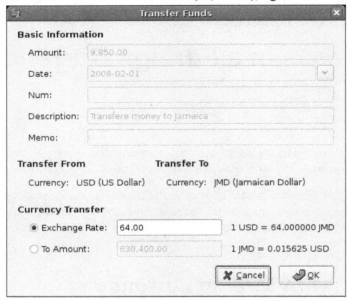

A dialog window where the exchange rate in a currency transaction is specified

As Exchange Rate, you enter 1 USD = 64 JMD, since this is the rate your bank gave. Press ok in the Transfer Funds (Edit Exchange Rate) window, and then save this split transaction. Below is how it now looks in the main Chart of Accounts.

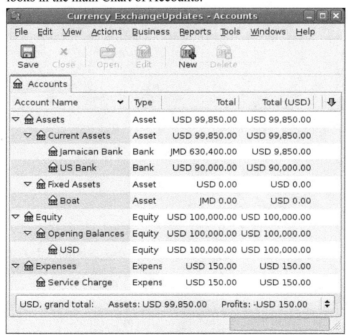

Chart of Accounts before purchasing the boat

You find the boat, and since it's a bargain at JMD 509,000 you decide to buy it. To record this transaction in GnuCash, you will need to enter a simple transaction in *Assets:Current Assets:Jamaican Bank* withdrawing 509,000 and transferring it to *Assets:Fixed Assets:Boat*

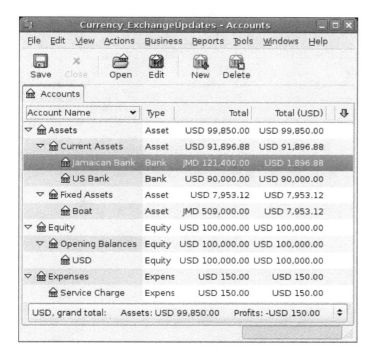

Chart of Accounts after purchasing the boat

The Chart of Accounts now reflects that your bank account has been reduced with the value of the boat (JMD 509,000), and that your Fixed Assets boat account has been increased with the same amount. If you also have turned on the CoA (Column Choice) "Total (USD)" you will see the corresponding value in USD. The USD value will always reflect the latest currency exchange rate you have either automatically or manually updated GnuCash with.

Purchasing foreign stocks

This example will show how to purchase stocks that are priced in a different currency than your normal currency.

Assume that you live in New York and therefore you have set the default currency to USD. You decide to purchase a stock traded in Hong Kong that is priced in HKD. You would also like to be able to track the various income and expense amounts per stock and broker.

You decide to purchase stock in the Beijing Airport (Hong Kong). (After all, the 2008 Olympics in Beijing have finished and the price has returned to Earth.)

Note

The above stock (Beijing Airport) has been chosen only as an example, and should not be taken as any kind of stock purchase advice.

You need to find out what the stock ticker is for this stock. To do this, you do a bit of investigation on the Internet, and in particular on *Yahoo! Finance - Ticker Symbol Lookup* [http://finance.yahoo.com/lookup] (http://finance.yahoo.com/lookup). This gives you the following:

• *Beijing Airport* has the Stock Symbol 0694.HK at Yahoo

Since we wanted to be able to track all various income and expense amounts, we come up with the following Account structure:

Assets:Investments:Brokerage Accounts:Boom:0694.HK   (Beijing Airport)
Assets:Investments:Brokerage Accounts:Boom:Bank   (HKD)
Equity:Opening Balances:HKD   (HKD)
Expenses:Commissions:Boom.0694.HK   (HKD)
Income:Investments:Dividend:Boom:0694.HK   (HKD)

The Chart of Accounts looks like this after creating all the needed accounts:

Chart of Accounts for international stocks

The stock definition can be seen in the Security Editor. (Tools+Security Editor)

International securities

If you have not moved money (HKD 50,000) into the brokerage's cash account (*Assets:Investments:Brokerage Account:Boom:Bank*), do so now, either using the Equity (HKD) account, or an existing bank account (Currency Transfer).

Let's assume that the stock price is HKD 3 per share. To record the purchase, open the brokerage's HKD cash account (*Assets:Investments:Brokerage Account:Boom:Bank*), and enter the following:

Buy Stocks
 Assets:Investments:Brokerage Account:Boom:Bank Withdrawal 50,000
 Expenses:Investments:Commission:Boom_HKD Deposit 500
 Assets:Investments:Brokerage Account:Boom:0694 Deposit 49,500 (16,500 shares)

If the exchange rate dialog box does not appear automatically, right-click on the stock row, and select Edit Exchange Rate. Enter the number of shares (16,500) as the To Amount.

Setting the number of shares in the Transfer Funds dialog

If you return to the Chart of Accounts, you will see the purchased shares reflected in the stock account's total.

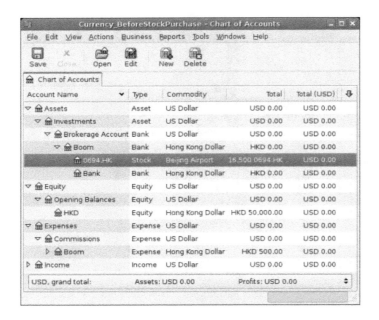

Chart of Accounts with some international stocks

However, as you can see, the USD totals may be zero if GnuCash doesn't have an exchange rate between USD and HKD. To fix this, go to Tools → Price Editor and click the Get Quotes button to automatically retrieve the exchange rates you need.

Note

This example shows how stock can be purchased in any currency by entering the transaction in the register of the cash account used to make payment. It is also possible to enter the purchase in the stock account's register, but proceed with caution! When doing it that way, the stock is assumed to be priced in the currency of the stock account's parent.

In this example, the stock account's parent (*Assets:Investments:Brokerage Account:Boom*) is denominated in HKD. Since this is same currency as the stock price, the purchase can be safely entered in the stock account's register.

Tracking Currency Investments (How-To)

Currency investment is when you decide to invest in different countries' currency, and hope that their currency will raise in value relative your own currency.

When you enter these transactions into GnuCash, you will have to decide on how much detail you would like to have.

If you are not interested in detail at all, a very simple account structure would be enough. Something like this;

    Assets:Investments:Currency:Bank (USD)
    Assets:Investments:Currency:XXX (XXX)

But, if you do want to be able to track the Capital Gains or Losses, as well as the various fees, you do need a bit more complexed layout. Something like this;

```
Assets:Investments:Currency:Bank              (USD)
Assets:Investments:Currency:Currency Bank:XXX    (XXX)
Expenses:Investments:Currency:Currency Bank:XXX   (XXX)
Income:Investments:Currency Bank:Capital Gains:XXX  (XXX)
```

Where XXX is the currency you are investing in.

Purchasing a currency investment

A typical purchase order might be something like this, seen from the *Assets:Investments:Currency:Bank*.

Table 10.1. Buying a currency with a Split Transaction Scheme

Account	Deposit	Withdrawal
Assets:Investments:Currency:Bank		Invested Amount
Expenses:Investments:Currency:Currency Bank:XXX	Exchange Fee	
Assets:Investments:Currency:XXX	Invested Amount - Exchange Fee	

You should get an Exchange Rate window popping up when you leave the last row in the split above (Currency Transaction). If this window does not pop up, right click on the row, and select Edit Exchange Rate. In the Exchange Rate window you specify the exchange rate you got from the bank.

Selling a currency investment

Entering a currency sale is done in the same way as a currency buy except that you are now transferring money from the Currency account to your Savings account (very similar to the section called "Selling Shares").

The proper recording of the currency sale *must* be done using a split transaction. In the split transaction, you must account for the profit (or loss) as coming from an *Income:Capital Gains* account (or *Expenses:Capital Loss*). To balance this income, you will need to enter the Currency asset twice in the split. Once to record the actual sale (using the correct amount and correct exchange rate) and once to balance the income profit (setting the amount to 0).

In short, a selling Currency transaction should look something like below, seen again from the *Assets:Investments:Currency:Bank*.

Table 10.2. Selling a currency with a Split Transaction Scheme

Account	Deposit	Withdrawal
Assets:Investments:Currency:Bank	Sold Amount - Exchange Fee	
Expenses:Investments:Currency:Currency Bank:XXX	Exchange Fee	
Assets:Investments:Currency:XXX		Sold Amount
Income:Investments:Currency Bank:Capital Gains:XXX	[LOSS]	PROFIT
Assets:Investments:Currency:XXX	PROFIT (with To Amount = 0)	[LOSS (with To Amount = 0)]

Reconciling Statements in a Foreign Currency (How-To)

Reconciling foreign statement are done in the same manner as when you reconcile your local bank statement. If you have created a Chart of Accounts structure which allows you to have the same Currency per account as your Reconcile Statement, it is actually exactly the same as reconciling your local bank statement, apart from the fact you might need a dictionary

If you have different currencies you might have to manually convert the amounts from one currency to another while you reconcile the accounts.

Putting It All Together (Examples)

In this Putting It All Together you will use quite a bit of what you have learned so far in this guide with a bit of a twist. The twist being a lot of different currencies.

Basic scenario

The following are the basic scenarios.

- You live in Australia and use AUD as our default currency

- You win the lottery as well as inherit some money

- You pay off your existing house loan

- You purchase some stock in Sweden using SEK (Ericsson B-Fria)

- You purchase some stock in HK using HKD (Beijing Airport)

- You purchase some stock in US using USD (Amazon)

- You lend some EURO to a friend (Peter)

- You borrow some money from a Japanese bank

- You buy a house in New Zealand

- You use a credit card in Australia

- You would like to have maximum control of your expenses

Note

Again these examples are not intended as valid and accurate advice. They are only to be considered as an example for the techniques used in GnuCash, and not as Investment Advice. Please consult a proper financial advisor for more information regarding international investments/loans.

Configure Accounts

This time let's start with a fresh and new GnuCash data file, so File → New File, and edit preferences (Edit → Preferences, GnuCash → Preferences on Mac OS X) to set Default Currency as AUD. Since you have decided to be able to track as much detail of your income and expenses as possible, the following account hierarchy could be used;

Assets:Current Assets:Savings Account   (AUD)

Opening Balance

You open the mail one morning, and to your enormous surprise find that you are the last living relative of a very distant relative who happened to be very rich. And so, now you are $500,000 AUD richer. That was not all though; another item in the mail states that you won the lottery, and got $250,000 AUD for that.

To record these transaction we need the following accounts

Equity:Lottery   (AUD)
Equity:Inheritance   (AUD)

The transactions you enter into your *Assets:Current Assets:Savings Account* should look like this.

Table 10.3. You come into some extra money

Account	Increase	Decrease
Equity:Lottery	$250,000	
Equity:Inheritance	$500,000	

And the Chart of Accounts looks like this after above transactions have been entered.

Chart Of Accounts after receiving some money

Purchase a house

At last you can afford to pay off that house loan you had to take some years ago (with a $50,000 deposit).

Assets:Fixed Assets:House   (AUD) $300,000
Liabilities:Loans:Mortgage   (AUD) $250,000

Expenses:Interest:Mortgage Interest   (AUD)
Equity:Opening Balance   (AUD) $50,000

After you have had a small chat with your Mortgage bank, they agree to let you pay it all off in one go, plus some interest (AUD 30,000). You should enter the following split transaction into *Assets:Fixed Assets:House* account.

Table 10.4. Paying of the house mortgage

Account	Increase	Decrease
Assets:Current Assets:Savings Account		280000
Expenses:Interest:Mortgage Interest	30000	
Liabilities:Loans:Mortgage	250000	

The *Liabilities:Loans:Mortgage* account Transaction Ledger looks like this after the transactions have been entered

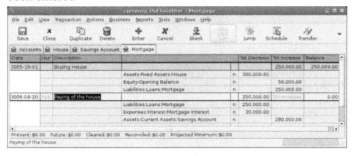

Transaction Ledger of the House Loan

Purchasing Stock

Since you quite suddenly have a lot of money in your bank account, you decide to visit a Financial Advisor, and after his recommendation (remember, this is fictional - not genuine stock purchase advice) you decide to purchase Telecommunication (Ericsson in Sweden), Beijing Airport (Hong Kong), and Amazon (USA).

The needed accounts to track these investments look like this:

Assets:Investments:Swedish Broker:ERIC.ST   (STOCK ERIC.ST Yahoo)
Assets:Investments:Swedish Broker:Bank   (SEK)
Assets:Investments:HK Broker:0694.HK   (STOCK 0694.HK Yahoo)
Assets:Investments:HK Broker:Bank   (HKD)
Assets:Investments:US Broker:AMZN   (STOCK AMZN Nasdaq)
Assets:Investments:US Broker:Bank   (USD)
Expenses:Investments:Commissions:Swedish Broker:ERIC.ST (SEK)
Expenses:Investments:Commissions:HK Broker:0694.HK   (HKD)
Expenses:Investments:Commissions:US Broker:AMZN   (USD)
Expenses:Investments:Currency Transfer   (AUD)

You decide to invest $100,000 into each stock, and to do this we first do a currency transaction to the various bank accounts associated with the stock.

The transaction you enter into your *Assets:Current Assets:Savings Account* should look like this.

Table 10.5. Transfer money to overseas with a multiple currency transaction split.

Account	Deposit	Withdrawal	Exchange Rate	Transaction Fee
Assets:Investments:Swedish Broker:Bank	1,000,000		5.5869	35
Assets:Investments:HK Broker:Bank	100000		5.8869	30
Assets:Investments:USD Broker:Bank	50000		0.7593	25

Now when there is some money in the various stock brokerage accounts, you ask each broker to buy shares of stock for the specified amount. Remember to execute the transaction from the bank account associated with the stock, and if the Exchange Rate window does not pop up, right click the row and manually select it. Enter the number of shares you purchase in the last entry (To Amount:).

Table 10.6. Purchasing oversea stocks

Stock Symbol	Number of shares	Amount	Commission
ERIC.ST	15000	270000	400
0694.HK	70000	280000	300
AMZN	1000	32000	25

As you can see in the Chart of Accounts, you have now purchased shares of stock in three different currencies (HK, USD, as well as in SEK), but the Chart of Account (as seen below) does not indicate how much they are valued in your home currency, AUD.

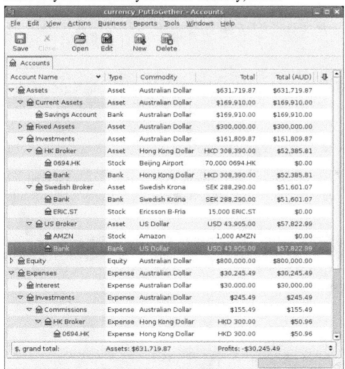

Some of the accounts in Chart of Accounts after the stock purchase

The next section will ensure you get the various exchange rates so that GnuCash can show your total worth in the local currency (AUD in this case),

Get the online quotes

To get the current exchange rates and stock quotes, go to Tools → Price Editor and then click on Get Quotes.

Lending money to a friend

Peter has run into some difficulties all the way over in Europe Land. Since he is a very dear pal of yours, you decide to help him out with a personal loan of 40,000 Euro.

Assets:Money owed to me:Euro:Peter   (Euro)
Income:Interest Income:Peter   (Euro)
Expenses:Bank Charge   (AUD)

This is a simple currency transaction from your Savings Account (AUD), to your Assets:Money owed to me:Peter (EURO) account. You got the exchange rate of 0.606161, which means you need to withdraw AUD 65,989.10, as well as pay the service fee of 35 AUD.

Buying property in New Zealand with a loan from Japan

Your long-time Japanese friend offers you a Japanese house loan if you purchase a property overseas, with only AUD 50,000 as deposit. After having discussed this with your Financial Advisor in Australia and gone through the various risks and benefits related to your situation, you decide to accept his offer.

Note

Again, this should not be taken as financial advice. Please consult with a registered financial advisor before undertaking investing (or speculating) in overseas markets, or local markets for that matter.

A word of warning might be of interest here, taking a loan overseas for a very low interest rate might seem like a very good deal. Do keep in mind though that the exchange rate might change and can change drastically. If you take a loan in your local currency, you only have to worry about the interest rate. If you take a loan overseas, you then have to worry about the interest rate and the exchange rate.

You found a nice small cottage in a small coastal town near Auckland which would be a perfect summer house, and you decide to use the money from Japan for this purpose.

We need the following accounts for this example;

Liabilities:Loans:Japan Loan   (JPY)
Expenses:Interest:Japan Loan   (JPY)
Expenses:Mortgage Adm Fees:Japan Loan   (JPY)
Assets:Current Assets:Japan Bank   (JPY)
Assets:Fixed Assets:NZ House   (NZ)

Table 10.7. Buying a NZ House Split Transaction

Account	Increase	Decrease
Assets:Fixed Assets:NZ House	300000 (NZD)	
Assets:Current Assets:Savings Account		50000 (AUD) (1.18926)
Liabilities:Loans:Japan Loan		28000000 (JPY) (0.0137609)
Expenses:Mortgage Adm Fees:Japan Loan	300000 (JPY) (0.0137609)	

Whats next?

As you have seen in the above examples you have only done the initial purchases. The rest, that is, various selling transactions and unrealized gains tracking is left for you to ponder.

Part III. Managing Business Finances

Table of Contents

Chapter 11. Business Introduction

The accounting needs of a business are quite different from that of a person. Businesses have customers that owe money, vendors which are owed money, employee payroll, more complex tax laws, etc. GnuCash offers business oriented features to facilitate these needs.

Accounts Receivable (A/R) are used by businesses to record sales for which they are not immediately paid. This is represented on the balance sheet as an asset, because the expectation is that you will receive payment soon.

Accounts Payable (A/P) record bills that businesses have received, but may not pay until later. This is represented on the balance sheet as a liability because you will have to pay for them.

A/R and A/P accounts are used primarily when you have a lot of bills and receipts flowing in and out, and do not want to lose track of them just because you do not pay or get paid right away. For most home users, A/R and A/P are too complicated to be worthwhile.

Chapter 12. Business Setup

To set up GnuCash to handle accounts receivable or accounts payable for a company, these preliminary steps must be done.

- Build an appropriate Account Hierarchy.

- Set up Tax Tables.

- Register the company in GnuCash.

- Set Business Preferences.

- Set up Billing Terms.

Account Setup

There are many different ways to set up a business account hierarchy. You can start with the Business Accounts setup which is available from the New Account Hierarchy assistant, or you could build one manually. To access the prebuilt Business Accounts, start GnuCash and click on File → New File and proceed until you see the list of available accounts, select Business Accounts.

The prebuilt Business Account hierarchy will not meet your needs exactly. You will need make adjustments for the hierarchy to function well with your particular situation. It should be close enough that it is recommended you begin with it.

To use GnuCash's integrated accounts receivable system, you must first set up an account (usually a sub-account under Assets) defined with account type *A/Receivable*. It is within this account that the integrated A/R system will place transactions.

To use GnuCash's integrated accounts payable system, you must first set up an account (usually a sub-account under Liabilities) defined with account type *A/Payable*. It is within this account that the integrated A/P system will place transactions.

Basic A/R and A/P Account Hierarchy:

```
-Assets
  -Accounts Receivable
  -Checking
-Expenses
 ...(as required)
-Income
  -Sales
-Liabilities
  -Accounts Payable
  -Tax
    -Tax on Purchases
    -Tax on Sales
```

You need to add additional accounts to this hierarchy for it to be useful.

Note

You do not need to create an individual A/R account for each customer. GnuCash keeps track of customers internally and provides per-customer reports based on the internal tracking. The same applies to A/P and vendors.

If you deal with customers in more than one currency you will need a separate *Accounts Receivable* account for each currency.

If you deal with vendors in more than one currency you will need a separate *Accounts Payable* account for each currency.

Transactions involving an Accounts Receivable or Accounts Payable account should not be added, changed or deleted in any way other than by using

- post/unpost bill/invoice/voucher or

- process payment

Tax Tables

Tax Tables can used to determine the tax for customer invoices (or vendor bills).

A tax table can be assigned to an invoice line or bill line.

Set up distinct tax tables for customers and vendors.

The default invoice line tax table can be assigned to each customer and the default bill line tax table can be assigned to each vendor.

The default tax table for new customers or new vendors can be specified in the *Book Options* window which can be accessed by File → Properties → Business tab.

Tax Tables are maintained using the *Sales Tax Table* editor which is accessed via menu Business → Sales Tax Table.

Figure 12.1. Tax Tables

Figure 12.2. New Sales Tax Table

- Name This is the tax table name.

- Type Either Percent % or Value $.

- Value This is the percentage or value depending on Type.

- Account This is the account to which tax will be posted. For tax collected from customers, this should probably be a Liability account as it must be payed to the government. For tax paid to vendors, if tax laws allow tax paid to vendors to offset tax collected from customers, this should probably also be a Liability account (even though it will usually have a debit balance) so that the net tax owed to the government can be easily observed.

  If you set up Tax on Purchases and Tax on Sales as subaccounts of Liabilities:Tax then the net tax will be rolled up and can be seen in the GnuCash Accounts tab.

  If unsure about tax law requirements, get professional advise.

Company Registration

After you have built the account structure and defined your tax tables, register the GnuCash file as belonging to your company. To register your company, select the Business tab in the Book Options window accessible by selecting File → Properties.

Figure 12.3. Company Registration

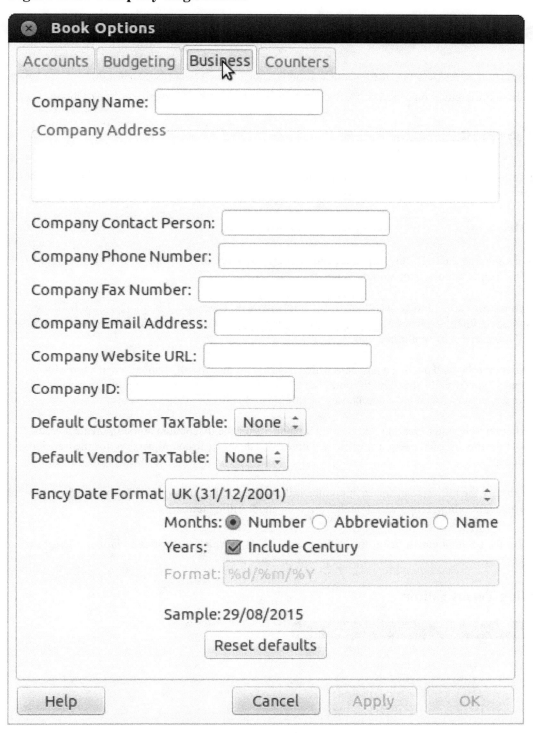

Here you can:

- Enter the name of your company along with contact information such as your phone number, fax number, e-mail address and website URL.

- Enter your company's tax payer id number in the Company ID field.

- Select default tax tables applicable to your most common customers and vendors.

Business Preferences

Set options on the Business tab of the GnuCash preferences, which is accessed via Edit → Preferences (GnuCash → Preferences on Mac OS X). See Help manual chapter 10.3.3 Business Book Options Tab.

Billing Terms

Billing Terms can be used to determine the payment due date and be a guide for determining discount for early payment of invoices (or vendor bills).

Note

As of GnuCash 2.6.7, Billing Terms are only partially supported. Date due is calculated using the Billing Terms but discount amount is not.

Discount for early invoice payment is not implemented. There are 2 ways this may be done, although neither is recommended, and professional advise should be used to confirm that regulations are being complied with:

- After creating and posting a payment which pays the invoice in full, manually edit the payment transaction (usually strongly discouraged) and split the payment to reduce it by the amount of the discount and a create a compensating split in an income (discount) account.

- Alternatively, after creating and posting a payment for the discounted amount, create a credit note for the discount using a specific negative sales income (discount) account for the transfer account.

You can specify the billing terms on each invoice/bill. Invoice billing terms will default from the customer billing terms. Bill billing terms will default from the vendor billing terms.

Billing Terms are maintained using the Billing Terms Editor which is accessed via menu Business → Billing Terms Editor.

Figure 12.4. Billing Terms Editor

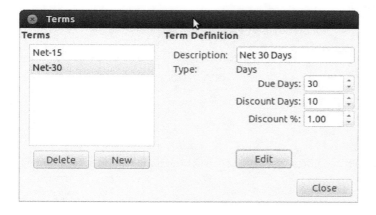

Figure 12.5. New Billing Term

- Name The internal name of the billing term. For some examples of billing term names and descriptions see http://wiki.gnucash.org/wiki/Terms.

- Description The description of the billing term, printed on invoices

- There are 2 types of billing terms, with different information to be entered

  - Type Days

    - Due Days The invoice or bill is due to be paid within this number of days after the post date

    - Discount Days The number of days after the post date during which a discount will be applied for early payment

    - Discount % The percentage discount applied for early payment

  - Type Proximo

    - Due Day The day of the month bills are due

    - Discount Day The last day of the month for the early payment discount

    - Discount % The discount percentage applied if paid early

    - Cutoff Day The cutoff day for applying bills to the next month. After the cutoff, bills are applied to the following month. Negative values count backwards from the end of the month.

Chapter 13. Accounts Receivable

Accounts Receivable (or A/R) refers to products or services provided by your company for which payment has not yet been received.

Initial Setup

Perform set up tasks listed in Chapter 12, *Business Setup*.

System Components

GnuCash has an integrated accounts receivable system. The transactions generated by the A/R system are recorded within the Accounts Receivable account. You generally do not work directly with this account. You generally work with the four integrated GnuCash A/R application components available through the Business → Customer sub-menu. These four components are:

- Customers are people or companies to whom you sell products or services on credit.

- Invoices represent the physical invoice you send to a customer to request payment. This invoice contains an itemized list of things you sold.

  In addition, GnuCash also has support for Credit Notes which represent the inverse of Invoices. A credit note is usually handed to a customer to correct items that were incorrectly invoiced or returned.

  Both document types will be set up using the same menu items. Credit notes were introduced starting with GnuCash stable release 2.6.0.

- Jobs (optional) is where you register Customer Jobs. Jobs are a mechanism by which you can group multiple invoices to a particular customer.

- Process Payments is used to register payments you received from a customer.

Customers

Customers are people or companies to whom you sell goods or services. They must be registered within the A/R system.

New

To register a new customer, enter the menu Business → Customer → New Customer. Fill in customer information, such as Company Name, Address, Phone, Fax, etc.

New Customer Registration Window

Find and Edit

To search for an existing customer, use the Business → Customer → Find Customer window. You select a customer to View/Edit from the results of the search. This window is also used to look up customers when creating invoices and processing payments.

Find Customer Window

If many customers match the search criteria you provide, the search can be refined by running an additional search within the current results. The current result set is searched when the Refine Current Search radio button is selected. In fact, GnuCash selects this option for you after you run the initial search.

If the customer you are searching for does not match the supplied search criteria, change the search criteria, click the New Search radio button and then the Find button. The relevant step is the New Search selection. If the customer is not in the result of the original search, and you only search within this set, the customer cannot be found, regardless of new search criteria.

Note

To return a list of all registered active customers, set the search criterion to matches regex, and place a single dot "." in the text field area. Make sure Search only active data is checked, then click Find. The regular expression "." means to match anything.

Invoices

An invoice is the paperwork you send to a customer to request payment for products or services rendered. GnuCash can generate and track invoices.

A credit note is the paperwork you send to a customer to correct products or services rendered that were incorrectly invoiced. GnuCash can generate and track credit notes via the same menu entries as invoices.

Note

This section applies to both invoices and credit notes. In order to avoid repeating everything twice and to keep the text easier to read it will refer only to invoices. You can apply it equally to credit notes. Only where the behaviour of credit notes differs from invoices this will be explicitly mentioned.

New

To send an invoice to a customer you must first create the new document. To create an invoice use Business → Customer → New Invoice. The New Invoice window must be filled in appropriately.

Creating a New Invoice

When you click the OK button, the Edit Invoice window opens.

Edit

From the Edit Invoice window you can enter an itemized list of goods and services you sold on this invoice in a manner similar to how the account register works. For credit notes you enter an itemized list of goods and services you refunded instead.

Edit Invoice Window

When you have finished entering all the items, you can Post and print the invoice.

Post

When you finish editing an invoice and are ready to print, you must Post the invoice. The invoice does not have to be posted immediately. In fact, you should only post an invoice when you are ready to print it. Posting an invoice places the transactions in an accounts receivable account.

Post Invoice Window

Find

To find an existing invoice, use the Business → Customer → Find Invoice menu item. From the results of the search, you can select an invoice to edit or view.

Note

Before you can edit a posted invoice, you will need to Unpost it.

One of the design goals in GnuCash's Account Receivable system was to allow different processes to get to the same state, so you can reach an invoice from different directions based on the way you think about the problem:

• You can search for the customer first, then list their invoices.

• You can search for invoices by number or by company name.

• You can list invoices associated with a customer job.

Print

After you post an invoice, you should print it and send it to your customer. To print an invoice use File → Print Invoice menu item.

```
Invoice #000001

Invoice Date: 04/19/06                    My Company
Due Date:    05/19/06                     9876 Second St.
                                          Othercity, SS 12345
                                          April 19, 2006
ABC Inc
123 First Ave.
Somecity, SS 12345

Reference: ABC Purchase Order # 12988
Terms: 30 Days - same as cash
```

Date	Description	Charge Type	Quantity	Unit Price	Discount	Taxable	Total
04/19/06	Nails	Material	1,000.00	$0.10	0.00%		$100.00
04/19/06	Hammer	Material	1.00	$500.00	5.00%		$475.00
Subtotal							$575.00
Tax							$0.00
Amount Due							$575.00

Thank you for your patronage

Invoice Print Output

Note

You can modify the appearance of the invoice, IE: add a company logo, etc. To do so, see the the section called "Changing the Invoice Appearance".

Invoices can also be printed from the main window by selecting Reports → Business Reports → Printable Invoice from the main menu. The resulting report window states that no valid invoice is selected. To select the invoice to print:

1. Use the Options *Toolbar* button or select Edit → Report Options from the main menu.

2. Select the General tab of the report options dialog.

3. Click the Select button next to the Invoice Number field.

4. Search for the invoice as usual.

You can also print invoices from within the Process Payment dialog. See the the section called "Process Payment" for instructions on how to do so.

Assign Starting Invoice Number

By default, GnuCash starts with invoice number 1 and increments from there. You can manually type an invoice number into the text box each time you create an invoice, but this gets tiring and sooner or later leads to duplicate numbers.

You can change the starting invoice number if it is important you. Use File → Properties, access the Counters tab, change the Invoice number value to be one less than your desired starting invoice number and click the OK button or the Apply button.

Customer Jobs

Customer Jobs are used to group multiple invoices and credit notes to the same customer. Use of the Customer Jobs feature is optional. The feature is useful when you have multiple jobs for the same customer, and would like to view all the invoices and credit notes related to a single job.

New Customer Job

To use customer jobs, you must create them using the Business → Customer → New Job menu item. You will see the New Job window.

To edit an existing customer job, use the Business → Customer → Find Job menu item. Select the desired job in the search results, and click the View/Edit Job button.

To select from the invoices and credit notes associated with a given job, use Business → Customer → Find Job menu item. Select the desired job in the search results and click the View Invoices button. A window listing invoices and credit notes associated with this job appears. Select an invoice or credit note and click the View Invoice button to open an invoice editor in the main application window.

Process Payment

Eventually, you will receive payment from your customers for outstanding invoices. To register these payments, use the Process Payment application found in Business → Customer → Process Payment.

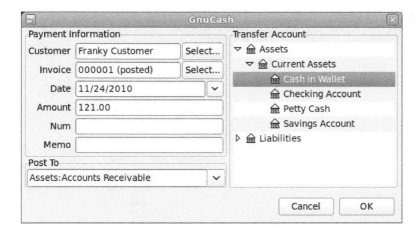

Process Payment Window

Changing the Invoice Appearance

The default Invoice style, as shown in the section called "Print", is fairly barren. The default invoice style leaves the top part of the form blank, so you can print on company letterhead paper. There are some things you can do to change invoice appearance.

Use File → Properties to enter your Company informations in the Business tab of the Book Options window. Some of the entered informations are printed on the right side of invoices.

To add a customized background, heading banner or logo to invoices, modify the invoice style sheets. To do this, go to Edit → Style Sheets and select the New button in the Select HTML Style Sheet window that will appear. You will then see a window like this:

The New Style Sheet window.

Give a Name to the new style sheet (e.g. Custom Invoice) and select the Fancy Template. When you click the OK button, the HTML Style Sheet Properties window is displayed. This window presents you five sections listed in the left pane: Colors, Fonts, General, Images, and Tables. The Colors section allows you to change the colors of various items of the invoice. The Fonts section lets you set fonts type and dimensions. The General section allows you to set the Preparer and Prepared for information, and to Enable Links. The Images section allows you to import graphics into the style sheet. The Tables section allows you to adjust the spacing around the tables which make up the invoice.

To include a company logo, banner heading and background image, use your favorite graphics application such as The Gimp or OpenOffice Draw to save the images in either GIF or PNG format. Then import them into the style sheet using the Images section described above.

Below is an example that imports all three types of images.

The HTML Style Sheets window with an example Background Tile, Heading Banner, and Logo.

Note

The images are placed in the invoice as follows. The Background Tile is tiled to become the background image, the Heading Banner goes to above the invoice text, and the Logo is placed in the upper left corner of the invoice to the left of the Heading Banner. You will probably have to try a few different sized images until you get the invoices to print nicely. Some sizing suggestions are that the Logo should be 1 square cm (~0.5 inch), and the Heading Banner should be 15 cm (~6 inches) wide and 1 cm (~0.5 inch) tall.

With the style sheet configured, when you print the invoice, you select the style sheet to use from the Options menu. Below is the resultant invoice after applying the style sheet demonstrated above.

The hideous invoice which results from the graphics selected in the style sheet.

Chapter 14. Accounts Payable

Accounts Payable (or A/P) refers to the accounting of products or services which a company has bought and needs to pay for.

Initial Setup

Perform set up tasks listed in Chapter 12, *Business Setup*.

System Components

GnuCash has an integrated accounts payable system. The transactions generated by the A/P system are placed within the Accounts Payable account, as a record of what occurs. Generally you do not directly work with this account but use the four integrated GnuCash A/P application components. The A/P components are available from the Business → Vendor sub-menu. These A/P components are:

- Vendors are people or companies from which you buy products or services on credit.

- Bills represent the physical bills vendors send to request payment from you. A bill contains an itemized list of things you purchased.

  In addition, GnuCash also has support for Credit Notes which represent the inverse of Bills. A credit note is usually received from a vendor to correct items that were erroneously billed or returned.

  Both document types will be set up using the same menu items.

- Jobs (optional) is where you register Vendor Jobs. Jobs are mechanism by which you can group multiple bills from a particular vendor.

- Process Payments is where you register payments to a vendor to whom you owe money.

The following sections introduce the individual Accounts Payable application components.

Vendors

A vendor is a company or person from whom you purchase goods or services. Vendors must be registered within the A/P system.

New

To register a new vendor, select the Business → Vendor → New Vendor menu item. Fill in general information about the vendor, such as Company Name, Address, Phone, Fax, etc. Below is a list of the other options:

This is what the New Vendor registration window looks like:

New Vendor Registration Window

Find and Edit

To search for an existing vendor, use the Business → Vendor → Find Vendor window. You select a vendor to View/Edit from the results of the search. This window is also used to look up a vendor when entering bills and processing payments.

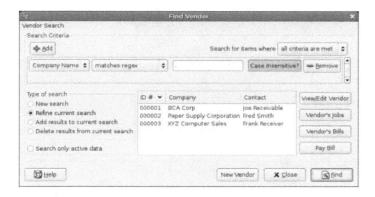

Find Vendor Window

If many vendors match the search criteria you provide, the search can be refined by running an additional search within the current results. The current result set is searched when the Refine Current Search radio button is selected. In fact, GnuCash selects this option for you after you run the initial search.

If the vendor you are searching for does not match the supplied search criteria, change the search criteria, click the New Search radio button and then the Find button. The relevant step is the New Search selection. If the vendor is not in the result of the original search, and you only search within this set, the vendor cannot be found, regardless of new search criteria.

Note

To return a list of all registered active vendors, set the search criterion to matches regex, and place a single dot "." in the text field area. Make sure Search only active data is checked, then click Find. The regular expression "." means to match anything.

Bills

A bill is a request for payment you receive from a vendor. GnuCash can track bills.

A credit note is the document you receive from a vendor to correct products or services rendered that you were incorrectly charged for on a bill. GnuCash can generate and track credit notes via the same menu entries as bills.

Note

This section applies to both bills and credit notes. In order to avoid repeating everything twice and to keep the text easier to read it will refer only to bills. You can apply it equally to credit notes. Only where the behaviour of credit notes differs from bills this will be explicitly mentioned.

New

When you receive a bill from a vendor and want to enter it into GnuCash, you must create a new bill. To create a new bill use the Business → Vendor → New Bill menu item, and fill in the resulting window appropriately.

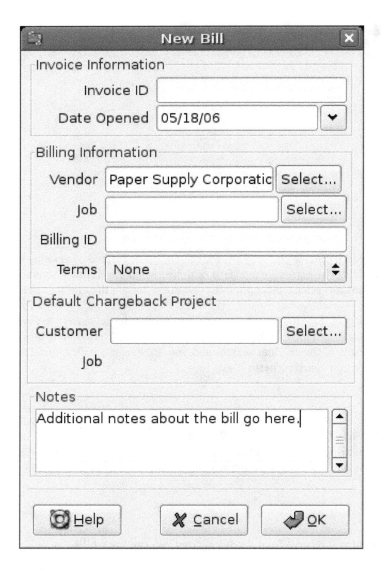

New Bill Registration Window

When you click the OK the Edit Bill opens.

Edit

From the Edit Bill window you can enter an itemized list of goods and services you purchased, in a manner similar to how the account register works. For credit notes you enter an itemized list of goods and services the vendor refunded instead.

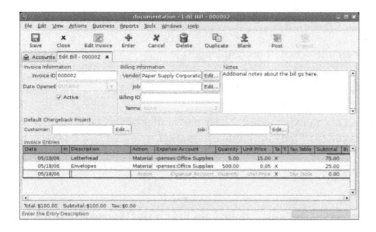

Edit Bill Window

When you have finished entering all the items, Post the bill.

Post

When you finish editing a bill, you should Post the bill. You do not have to post the bill, you can close it and return to it later. You have to post the bill eventually. Posting a bill places its transactions into an accounts payable account. The Post Bill window appears and asks you to enter information:

Post Bill Window

Find

To find an existing bill, use the Business → Vendor → Find Bill menu item. From the results of the search, you can select a bill to edit, or view.

Note

Before you can edit a posted bill, you will need to Unpost it.

Note

There are other ways to access an existing bill. These are similar to accessing invoices for your customers. See the section called "Find" for more information.

Vendor Jobs

Vendor Jobs are used to group multiple bills and credit notes from a single vendor. Use of the vendor jobs feature is optional. The feature is useful when you have multiple jobs for the same vendor, and would like to view all the bills and credit notes for a single job.

To use vendor jobs, you must create them using the Business → Vendor → New Job menu item. You will see the New Job window.

New Vendor Job

To edit an existing vendor job, use the Business → Vendor → Find Job menu item. Select the desired job in the search results, and click the View/Edit Job button.

To select from the bills associated with a given job, use Business → Vendor → Find Job menu item. Select the desired job in the search results and click the View Invoices button. A window listing bills and credit notes associated with this job appears. Select a bill or credit note and click the View Invoice button to open a bill editor in the main application window.

Process Payment

Eventually, you need to pay your bills. To do so, use the Process Payment application found in Business → Vendor → Process Payment.

Below is the GnuCash Accounts Receivable payment window.

Process Payment Window

Chapter 15. Payroll

Payroll is a financial record of wages, net pay, paid vacations, and deductions for an employee. This chapter demonstrates how to track payroll using GnuCash

Basic Concepts

Payroll is a financial record of wages, net pay, paid vacations, and deductions for an employee. Basically, anything that relates to giving money or benefits to an employee. Payroll is one of the more complex tasks in accounting, because there are many different accounts, people, and agencies involved in paying salaries.

Payroll is typically accounted for as an expense. Sometimes accountants "store" some payroll expenses in a short term liability account. This is useful for things such as payroll taxes, which may be paid at a different time than the employee. The employee might get paid biweekly, while taxes are paid quarterly. This chapter presents a methodology which expenses payroll immediately for salaries, but stores taxes in liability accounts.

Note

GnuCash does not have an integrated payroll system. While you can track payroll expenses in GnuCash, the calculation of taxes and deductions has to be done outside of GnuCash.

Account Setup

Local tax law must be considered when setting up accounts. Because there are many different ways payroll taxes are handled throughout the world, this section presents a very simple structure. From this, you should be able to adapt your particular payroll deductions setup.

Assume that you must pay 2 taxes, Tax1 and Tax2 and that each has an employee contributed and an employer contributed component.

The employee's salary and these two taxes are expense accounts. The tax components are liability accounts. The tax liability accounts are where you accumulate the taxes withheld for all of your employees. The taxes are later paid to the appropriate government agency.

Simple Payroll Account Layout:

```
-Assets
  -Checking
-Liabilities
  -Tax1  (short term "storage" account)
  -Tax2  (short term "storage" account)
-Expenses
  -Salaries
  -Tax1
  -Tax2
```

Note

Resist the temptation to create per-employee sub-accounts to track individual salaries. Creating a sub-account for each employee leads to unmanageably large lists of accounts. Imagine the account structure after a few years of employees coming and going. It is much simpler to keep all of your employees' payroll records within a single account (*Expenses:Salaries* for example) and use reports to view per-employee information.

Protocol

GnuCash does not have an integrated payroll system. GnuCash can track your payroll expenses, but you need to develop a payroll protocol and perform the calculations outside of GnuCash, in a spreadsheet for example. In this section, one such protocol is presented. You can use the sample protocol as a model.

Step 1: Deductions list

The first step to the payroll protocol is to create a list of all the possible taxes and deductions for each employee. Each entry should include definitions and formulas for calculating each value. Once the protocol is established it needs to be changed only when payroll laws or tax rates change.

In the proposed scenario, such a list would look like this:

- *E_GROSS_SALARY* - Employee gross salary
- *E_TAX1* - Employee contribution to tax1 (X% of E_GROSS_SALARY)
- *E_TAX2* - Employee contribution to tax2 (X% of E_GROSS_SALARY)
- *C_TAX1* - Company contribution to tax1 (X% of E_GROSS_SALARY)
- *C_TAX2* - Company contribution to tax2 (X% of E_GROSS_SALARY)

Note

The employee's net salary (E_NET_SALARY) is defined as E_GROSS_SALARY - E_TAX1 - E_TAX2 and need not be placed in this list since it is composed of items that already exist.

Place the actual formulas for calculating each deduction in this list. Sometimes these formulas are quite complex, and sometimes they simply say "look it up in table XYZ of the tax codes".

Notice that you can calculate some interesting values using the above definitions. One such value is the total cost to the company: E_GROSS_SALARY + C_TAX1 + C_TAX2.

Step 2: Create the Transaction Map

When you record payroll in GnuCash, do so with a single split transaction. This split transaction populates the appropriate expense and liability accounts. If you need to look the payroll details at a later time, open the split transaction.

With the deductions list from above, an employee split transaction map can be generated. Each of the items in the list is mapped to a GnuCash account.

Table 15.1. Transaction Map

Account	Increase	Decrease
Assets:Checking		E_NET_SALARY
Expenses:Salaries	E_GROSS_SALARY	
Liabilities:Tax1		E_TAX1

Account	Increase	Decrease
Liabilities:Tax2		E_TAX2
Expenses:Tax1	C_TAX1	
Liabilities:Tax1		C_TAX1
Expenses:Tax2	C_TAX2	
Liabilities:Tax2		C_TAX2

Note that the C_TAX1 and C_TAX2 components have entries in the both the liability and expense accounts. The company component of each tax is expensed at the time of payroll, but remains a liability until taxes are due.

Step 3: Pay the Employee

Go to the account from which the employee will be paid, for example your *Assets:Checking* account. Open a split transaction and enter the real values using the Transaction Map above as a guide. Repeat this for all employees.

Tip

This manual process is tedious, especially if you have a large number of employees.

One GnuCash tool you certainly want use when entering employee payroll is duplicate transaction (use the Duplicate *Toolbar* button). This saves you from having to enter all the transaction splits for each employee. You still need to change the amounts of money to match each employee's real payroll values, but you will not have to build the split for each employee.

If payroll transactions do not change significantly every pay period, you can also use the duplicate transaction feature to duplicate each employee's most recent payroll transaction for the current pay period. If you find you are doing so all the time, read about the Schedule Transactions feature and save even more time!

Step 4: Pay the Government

The final thing to do is to pay the taxes to the government. The liability accounts have been collecting the taxes for various government agencies, and periodically you need to send a check to the government to pay this charge. To do so, you simply enter a 2 account transaction in (for example) your checking account to pay off the tax liability. The transaction is between the checking account and the liability account, no expense account is involved. The expense accounts are charged at the time the tax liability is recorded.

Example

Using the account setup seen previously, let's go through an example. Assume that there are 2 employees (E1 and E2) which each earn $1000 per month gross salary. The employee contribution to Tax1 and Tax2 are 10% and 5% respectively. The company contribution to Tax1 and Tax2 are 15% and 10% each on top of the employees gross salary.

Staring with $50k in the bank, and before doing any payroll, the account hierarchy looks like this:

Payroll Initial Setup

Build Protocol

The deductions list for employee 1:

- *E_GROSS_SALARY* - Employee gross salary - *$1000*

- *E_TAX1* - Employee contribution to tax1 - *$100* (10% of E_GROSS_SALARY)

- *E_TAX2* - Employee contribution to tax2 - *$50* (5% of E_GROSS_SALARY)

- *C_TAX1* - Company contribution to tax1 - *$150* (15% of E_GROSS_SALARY)

- *C_TAX2* - Company contribution to tax2 - *$100* (10% of E_GROSS_SALARY)

Table 15.2. Transaction Map for Employee 1

Account	Increase	Decrease
Assets:Checking		$850 (E_NET_SALARY)

Account	Increase	Decrease
Expenses:Salaries	$1000 (E_GROSS_SALARY)	
Liabilities:Tax1		$100 (E_TAX1)
Liabilities:Tax2		$50 (E_TAX2)
Expenses:Tax1	$150 (C_TAX1)	
Liabilities:Tax1		$150 (C_TAX1)
Expenses:Tax2	$100 (C_TAX2)	
Liabilities:Tax2		$100 (C_TAX2)

Pay an Employee

Now, enter the first split transaction for employee 1 in the checking account. The split transaction looks like this:

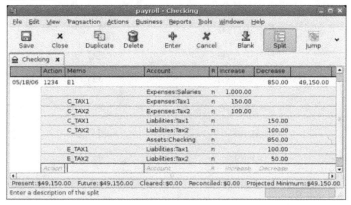

Employee 1 Split Transaction

Tip

When paying employees, enter only the employee name in the Description area. If you decide to use GnuCash's check printing capabilities, the check is automatically made out to the correct employee. If you want to record other information in the transaction besides the employee name, use the Notes area, available when viewing the Register in double-line mode.

Repeat this for the second employee, which leaves the account hierarchy looking like this:

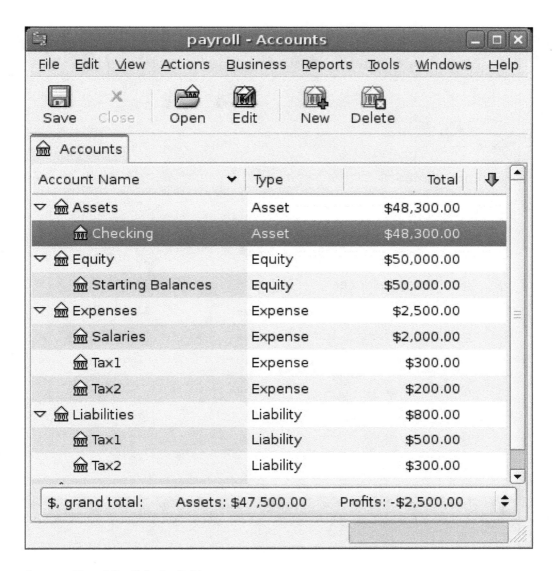

Account Tree After Salaries Paid

Pay the Government

The *Liabilities:Tax1* and *Liabilities:Tax2* accounts continue to track how much you must pay to the government agencies responsible for each. When it is time to pay these agencies, make a transaction from the checking account to the liability accounts. No expense accounts are involved. The main account will then appear like this for this example:

Accounts After Paying Government

Chapter 16. Budgets

This chapter explains how to create and use budgets with GnuCash.

Basic Concepts

A budget is a tool for estimating expected income and expenses. You can use it to help you plan how you intend for your finances to change over a period of time, and to examine how your actual financial transactions for the period compare to your planned transactions.

The budgeting concept is quite general, so GnuCash offers a budgeting tool that is both simple and flexible. You, the user, have to decide how complex or simple you want to make your budget. This guide will help you make some of those decisions.

Terminology

There are a few helpful terms listed below that will be used to discuss budgeting.

- *Budget* - A financial plan describing the expected revenues and/or disbursements for a particular time period

- *Cash Budget* - A budget planning for expected cash receipts and cash disbursements. This type of budget tracks cash flow -- where your money comes from, where it goes, and, of course, how much.

- *Expense Budget* - A budget chiefly for planning what you spend your money on. This type of budget tracks your expenses. It is typically not concerned with things like appreciation or repayment of liabilities. However, it would account for interest charges. For example, if you buy $100 worth of groceries with your credit card, you incur an $100 expense for groceries, and a $100 liability to your credit card company. When you pay the credit card bill for $110, you are incurring an additional interest expense of $10. An expense budget plans for the transaction of buying the groceries and paying the interest, but not the transaction of repaying the credit card company.

- *Capital Budget* - A budget that describes a plan for paying for a large future expense, often through a combination of saving and borrowing money. Note: Capital budgets can sometimes get quite complex because they can try to answer the question "Can we afford to do such-and-such?" by exploring various hypothetical scenarios that can involve hypothetical accounts.

- *Budget Period* - The period of time during which the plan is expected to take place. The most common budget periods are annual and monthly. Sometimes, you may budget for several consecutive periods at once, for convenience or for finer-grained planning. For example, an annual budget may include 12 monthly budget periods.

Creating a Budget

Even before you begin to make a budget, it's important to have given some thought to your account hierarchy. For example, if you want to budget a certain amount for your electric bill and a certain amount for your water bill, you can't have only an *Expenses:Utilities* account. Your accounts must be at least as specific as your budget.

Choose Which Accounts To Budget For

The first step in creating a budget is to decide what it is you want to plan for. This decision will affect which accounts you include in your budget. For example, if you are only interested in tracking your expenses, you may create an expense budget by only entering amounts for expense accounts. On the other hand, if you want to track all of your cash flow, you may create a cash flow budget by entering amounts for asset, liability, income and expense accounts.

Before you begin to create your budget, you need to make two decisions: What accounts do I want to budget for? and When do I want my budget to be for? You can always change your mind later, after you've created a budget, but you need to start with something.

Tip

As a rule of thumb, if you mostly care about *what* you spend your money on, you may want to make an expense report. If you're also concerned about having enough money in the right places at the right times, you may want to use a cash-flow budget.

Choosing a Budget Period

Before creating a budget you must also decide what period of time you want to plan for. The most common budget periods are monthly and annual. If you want your budget to plan for changes in financial patterns over time, then you should include multiple budget periods in your budget. For example, if you want to plan on having higher utility expenses in the winter than in the summer, then you might break your annual budget into 4 quarters or even 12 months, and budget a higher value for the winter periods than for the summer periods.

Getting Started

To create your first budget click on Actions → Budget → New Budget. You will immediately see a new budget with the default settings and no entries. Then click on the Options button. The most important options are the budget period and the number of periods. For the budget period, choose the beginning date and the smallest period of time that you want to plan for. Then, for the number of periods, choose how many periods you want to plan for.

The budget page now shows a list of accounts with a column for each budget period. The date shown in the title of each column is the beginning of that budget period.

Entering Budget Values

Now, you must enter the budget values - the amounts that you expect the account balances to change during the budget period. There are two ways to enter budget values. The first way is to simply click on the cell and enter an amount.

If you have past transactions recorded in GnuCash, the second way is to let GnuCash estimate the budget values by looking at those transactions. First, select the accounts you want GnuCash to estimate. Then click on the Estimate *Toolbar* button. In the Estimate Budget Values dialog, select the date past which GnuCash should look for past transactions. GnuCash will start at that date and look forward for the duration of your budget. For example, if you are making an annual budget, and you select Jan. 1, 2005, GnuCash will look at all the transactions in that account from Jan. 1, 2005 through Dec. 31, 2005.

Budget Reporting

You've already done the hardest part - creating your budget. But now you want to know how your actual financial transactions compare to your plan. You need to run the Budget Report.

Click on Reports → Budget → Budget Report. For each account, the Budget Report will show the budgeted and the actual amounts in two adjacent columns for each period in the budget. If you have created multiple budgets, you can use the Budget Report Options to select which budget to use in the report.

Two other types of budget reports are commonly used in the small business setting. They are the *Budgeted Income Statement* and the *Budgeted Balance Sheet*.

Budgeted Income Statement

The budgeted income statement is similar to the income statement. Both show the revenues and expenses for a given period as well as the profit, which is the difference revenue - expenses. The income statement is based on historical data, but the *budgeted* income statement is based on the predictions made in the budget.

Budgeted Balance Sheet

The budgeted balance sheet is similar to the balance sheet. Both show the assets, liabilities, and equity. The difference is that the balance sheet is based on historical data, and the *budgeted* balance sheet is based on the predictions made in the budget.

Chapter 17. Other Assets

General Concepts

This chapter presents many additional accounting treatments for frequently encountered business and less-frequently found personal activities that need recording in accounting books. The explanations below cover both the description and purpose of the activity, and they include also the usual accounting treatments (bookings or recordings) for these transactions.

These concepts have evolved over centuries of experience by those keeping accounting records and will help you maximize your record keeping's utility and meaningfulness.

This section introduces categorization of assets in the balance sheet based on time or the asset's useful life (current and long-term). Sometimes assets are also considered from the standpoint of their *liquidity*, which is regarded as how close or distant the asset is from being turned into cash. Near-cash assets are relatively quickly converted to cash (e.g., accounts receivable), while assets requiring rather a long time to convert to cash are considered to be relatively *fixed* in their non-cash state (e.g., heavy equipment, buildings, land). (Fixed does not mean they were repaired!)

You should find that current assets parallel those with more liquidity, while long-term and fixed assets are those with much less liquidity. Finally, below you will find a few assets that could be either current or long-term based on the nature of the facts constituting them.

Other Assets Described

Current Assets

Current Assets are those activities whose normal expected life would be one year or less. Such activities could be tracking reimbursable expenses, travel advances, short-term loans to a friend or family member, prepaid expenses, annual insurance premium amortization, and so on. The individual entity could have many other kinds of short term activities that reflect what it is doing. (These asset types are explained individually below.)

Long-term (Fixed) Assets

Long-term (Fixed) Assets are those activities whose normal expected life exceeds one or more years. This grouping covers both tangible and intangible assets. Examples of tangible assets are land, buildings, and vehicles (cars, trucks, construction equipment, factory presses, etc.) Intangible assets include such things as patents, copy rights, goodwill, etc. Because the lives of some of these assets show wear and tear and deterioration in value over time, businesses and individuals can allow for that diminution in value by calculating depreciation on such assets. For example, land normally does not depreciate, but buildings do, as do equipment and vehicles. (These asset types are explained individually below.)

Current Assets

This section explains short-term receivables, reimbursable expenses, travel advances, prepaid premiums, prepaid rent, suspense or wash accounts.

Short-term Receivables

This kind of account is useful to reflect an agreement made with someone you trust. Suppose you lent someone $500 and he agreed to repay you $50 a month. If he paid on time, the loan you made would be paid off within a year, which is why it is classified as a short-term receivable. So you could record that loan initially in this account tree: *OtherAssets:Current Assets:LoanToJoe.* At the time you give him the money: your entry is debit (increase) LoanToJoe $500 and credit (decrease) Bank $500. Each time you receive Joe's payment you record $50 debit (increase) to Bank and credit (decrease) LoanToJoe.

Tip

Don't become confused by the use of the word "Loan". "Loan-To" is the tipoff that you really have a receivable, that is, you will receive from Joe, the money you previously loaned. Until he actually pays the money owed you, you reflect his debt in your books by an account describing your expectation–you will receive the money owed you, hence the word "receivable".

Reimbursable Expenses

This kind of activity is one in which you spend your own money on behalf of someone else (your employer, perhaps) and later you receive repayment of what you spent. The case might be a business trip. The employer has a policy of covering (paying for) all authorized expenses. After the trip is over, the employee submits a report listing dates and amounts spent with receipts for all the expenditures. The employer reviews the report and pays for all items that it considers as having a valid business reason. (Normally, employees know in advance what the employer will reimburse, so only those items are recorded as a reimbursable expense on the employee's books.)

Because a business trip can involve different kinds of expenditures (air travel, lodging, transportation at the destination, etc.), different kinds of expenditures would be recorded in the one account as long as the expenditures all related to the same trip. In other words, if a second trip is made before the first is fully settled, a second account for a different event could be set up. It would make sense to do this, if it would help to keep separate all the details of one trip from those of another. It is up to the person making the trip to decide how much trouble it would be to put separate trips in separate accounts or to put them all in the same account. The trip taker should remember that the account must be reconciled in order to know with certainty that all expenses have been reimbursed.

Recording the expenditures on the trip would be much the same. That is, if you paid trip expenses by cash you would debit (increase) the reimburseable expense account for the money paid in cash, because it is a receivable to you until it has been reimbursed to you. The credit offsetting your expenditure would decrease the account that shows the cash in your pocket or the account from which you drew the cash for the payment made. If you paid by credit card, the debit side would be the same as just described, but the credit would be an increase to the credit card company account on your books.

When you received your reimbursement, then the journal entry (or transaction) to record receipt of the funds from the employer would be: debit (increase) Bank for the check amount and credit (decrease) the reimbursable expense account for the check amount.

If it turns out that the reimbursable expense account is not zero balance after processing the employer's payment, then it means that there is a difference between you and the employer in handling the expense, which needs to be investigated. If the balance is a debit (a positive balance), your account has some money that was not reimbursed. If the balance is a credit (a negative balance), you were paid for more than what you recorded as due you. In both of those situations you should reconcile the difference between what you recorded and what was paid. That effort should disclose exactly what is causing the discrepancy. You will need to contact the employer's bookkeeper to know what was paid, if the reimbursement check was not accompanied by a detailed list of the items being paid you.

In the event the employer refused to reimburse you for an expenditure, that effectively makes it your expense. In that case, you would make this entry: debit (increase) your own Expense (appropriately named) and credit (decrease) the Reimbursable Expense account. That entry should result in a zero balance in the Reimbursable Expense account. If not, reconcile until you identify the difference.

Tip

Sometimes there are small differences that don't match an individual entry. In those cases divide the amount by 2 or by 9. If the unresolved amount is divisible by two, it suggests that both you and the employer entered the item in the same manner: both as debits or both as credits. If it is divisible by 9, then likely one of you transposed adjoining numbers; e.g., one entered 69 and the other entered 96. If the difference is divisible neither by 2 or by 9, then it could be that more than one error is present.

Travel Advances

These are very similar to Reimbursable Expenses. The difference is that someone gives you money first; you spend it, and then you give a report accounting for what you spent it on. The report is supported by invoices establishing who, what, where, when, and how much for each expenditure. In the Reimbursable Expense case, you spent your money first and later recovered it.

In the Travel Advance case when you receive the advance, you record on your books this entry: debit (increase) Bank for the travel advance amount received (say, $500); credit (increase) the short-term liability Travel Advance ($500). This is a liability, because you are not gifted with the money, but only loaned it for the purpose of having funds to spend when doing the employer's business.

Frequently, the way these monetary arrangements work is that at the beginning of for example a salesperson's employment, he or she receives the advance and monthly (or more frequently) turns in a report about who, what, where, when, and how much he spent. The money in the report is reimbursed if approved.

During the period after receiving the advance and before filing a request for reimbursement report, the salesperson can record his or her expenditures into the advance liability account. In that case, the balance in the account will show how much of the advance has not yet been spent (assuming the Travel Advance balance is a credit). If no mistakes have been made and all expenses are approved, then the sum of the unspent account balance and the reimbursing check amount will equal the original travel advance amount.

It makes sense for the salesperson to record the travel expenses to this advance account (and not to his or her own expense accounts), because the money is being spent on behalf of the employer, for the employer's authorized expenses. It is not the employee's own money, and therefore not his or her own expense.

When the salesperson receives the report reimbursement (say, $350), he or she debits (increases) Bank, and credits (increases) again the Travel Advance liability account, assuming that previously he or she had been recording expenditures to the travel advance account. Tracking activity in this manner causes the account to always show the amount that is owed the employer.

See the section called "Reimbursable Expenses" above for what to do if the employer does not accept an item the employee put on the travel advance reimbursement request report. The difference resolution effort is essentially the same for both types of accounts.

Prepaid Premiums or Prepaid Rent

Some types of expenses are usually billed as semi-annual or annual amounts. For example, the insurance industry will bill home insurance annually, while car insurance premiums can be annual or semi-annual. For those that pay an amount that covers several months or a full year, the proper accounting treatment is to reflect in each accounting period the amount that expresses the benefit applying to that period.

In the case of someone who pays a full-year's insurance premium at the beginning of the insurance period, the entry to record this is debit (increase) Prepaid Insurance Premium for say, $1,200, and credit (decrease) Bank for $1,200.

Then a monthly recurring journal entry (scheduled transaction) is created that debits (increases) Insurance Expense $100 and credits (decreases) Prepaid Insurance Premium $100. This technique spreads the cost over the periods that receive the insurance coverage benefit. Businesses following generally accepted accounting practices would normally use this technique, especially if they had to present financial statements to banks or other lenders. Whether individuals do depends on the person and how concerned they are to match cost with benefit across time periods. Another factor influencing use of this technique would be the number of such situations the person encounters. It is relatively easy to remember one or two, but more difficult if having to manage 10 to 20. You would set up as many or as few as proved useful and important to you.

Suspense or Wash Accounts

The purpose of these accounts is to provide a device to track "change of mind" situations. The objective of these accounts is to provide a temporary location to record charges and credits that are not to be included permanently in your books of record. When the transactions reflected in these accounts have been fully completed, Wash/Suspense accounts will normally carry a zero balance.

For example, say in the grocery store you see canned vegetables on sale, so you buy 6 cans at $1 per can. Say that the total purchases were $50. When you come home and are putting things in the cupboard you discover you already had 12 cans. You decide to return the 6 you just bought. Some persons in this situation would charge (increase) the whole bill to Grocery Expense; and when they returned the cans, they would credit (decrease) Grocery Expense. That is one way of handling that. The effect of this method is to leave recorded on your books the cost of items that you really did not purchase from a permanent standpoint. It is only when the items have actually been returned and the vendor's return receipt has also been recorded that the distortion this method generates will then be removed.

Actually, there are several treatments, depending on when and how the original transaction was booked/recorded and when you decided to return the items purchased. Basically, did you change your mind before you recorded the transaction or after doing so?

If you decided to return the items after recording the purchase transaction, you may originally have charged Grocery Expense for the full amount ($50) of all items. In that scenario, what you kept and the amount of the items to be returned were grouped into one account. You could edit the original transaction and restate the amount charged to the Grocery Expense account to be the difference ($44) between the total paid ($50) for groceries and the value of the items to be returned. That leaves the returned-item value as the amount ($6) you should record to the Suspense account.

Obviously, if you decided to return items before you recorded your purchase, then you would book the original entry as a charge to Grocery Expense for the amount kept ($44) and as a charge to Suspense for the amount returned ($6). The off-setting credit ($50) to cash or credit card is not affected by these treatments.

When there are several persons shopping and at different vendors, there can be a case where there are several returns happening at once and in overlapping time frames. In that case the Wash Account is charged (increased) at time of changing the mind, and either Bank or Credit Card is credited. When the return occurs, the reverse happens: Bank or Credit Card is debited for the cash value of the returned items and the Wash/Suspense Account is credited in the same amount.

If the wash account has a non-zero balance, scanning the debit and credit entries in the account will show the non-matched items. That is, debits not matched by offsetting credits indicate items intended to be returned but not actually returned yet. The reverse (credits not matched by offsetting debits) indicates that returns were made but the original charge was not recorded in the Wash Account.

These differences can be cleared up by returning unreturned items or recording charges (debits) for items already returned. The mechanics of doing that likely will be finding the original expense account the item was charged to and making an entry like: debit Wash Account, credit original expense. It also could be as described above where the original recording is adjusted by adding a charge to Wash/Suspense account and decreasing the amount charged to the original account.

Short or Long-term Assets

This section explains why some types of assets may be short or long-term and presents an example.

An example is deposits (e.g., utility, rental, security). If the deposit agreement contains a provision to recover the deposit at the end of a year, the treatment could be that of a short-term asset. However, when the agreement is that the deposit holder returns the funds only upon successful inspection at the end of the relationship, then at the start of the relationship or agreement, the person paying the deposit has to decide whether to write it off as a current expense or to track it for eventual recovery at the end of the agreement (not infrequently, moving to a new location).

Whichever decision is made, the accounting treatment is to debit (increase) expense (assuming the write-off decision) or debit (increase) Deposits Receivable (assuming the intent is to recover the deposit in the future) and credit (decrease) Bank for the amount of the deposit (if paid by cash) or credit (increase) credit card if paid using that payment method.

Long-term (Fixed) Assets

This section illustrates long-term assets (those whose useful lives exceed a year) and discusses these types: land, buildings, leasehold improvements, intangibles, vehicles and other equipment.

Land

Land is not a wasting asset. That is, it does not get used up over time and rarely suffers damage such that it loses value. For that reason, it usually is recorded at cost at the time of purchase. Appreciation in its value over decades is not recorded and is not recognized in any way on the books of the owner. It is only after land has been sold that sale price and purchase cost are compared to calculate gain or loss on sale.

Land is frequently sold/purchased in combination with structures upon it. That means that the cost has to become separated from the cost of structures on it. Land valuation is usually part of the transfer of ownership process and its value is shown on the purchase documents separately from that of any structures it supports.

Land values shown on purchase documents frequently arise from the process of value determination managed by assessors whose job it is to assign values to land for tax purposes. Local and regional areas of a state or province use the values determined by assessors in their tax formulas, which provide revenues for local and regional governing authorities to finance their required community services.

Should land be acquired in a situation not subject to a history of land valuation by a formal valuation system, then the purchaser can appeal to real estate agents and an examination of recent sale transactions for information that would allow calculating a reasonable amount to express the value of the land.

Buildings

Buildings are the man-made "caves" in which much of life's human interaction occurs. These structures are wasting assets, because in their use they or their components gradually wear. Over time they begin to lose some of their function and they can suffer damage due to planetary elements or human action.

Accepted accounting practice is to record the cost of the building determined at time of ownership transfer (purchase) or at conclusion of all costs of construction. Because buildings are frequently used for decades, and due to the need to be able to calculate gain or loss on sale, accounting practice preserves the original cost by not recording declines in value in the account containing the original purchase or construction cost.

Instead, the depreciation technique is used to show (in the balance sheet) the structure's net book value (original cost reduced by accumulated depreciation). Depreciation is a separate topic treated elsewhere in this Guide.

Leasehold Improvements

When a business does not own the building where it operates, and instead has a long-term lease, it is not uncommon for the business tenant to make improvements to the premises so that the structure obtains both function and appearance that enhances conducting its business activities.

In these cases, the expenditures that the business incurs are recorded in a Leasehold Improvements account: increase (debit) Leasehold Improvements, decrease (credit) Bank or increase (credit) a suitable liability account (which could be a liability to a contractor or a bank or a credit card, etc.).

Vehicles or Equipment

Vehicles or Equipment of all kinds usually last for several years, but their useful lives are much shorter than that of assets that have little movement in their functioning. Because they do wear out over time, common accounting practice in business is to record depreciation using life spans and depreciation methods appropriate to the nature and use of the asset. Frequently, the life and depreciation methods chosen are influenced by what is permitted per national tax regulations for the kind of asset being depreciated.

Usually, businesses depreciate their assets. Individuals can do so as well to the degree that taxing authorities permit. Very wealthy persons employ accountants and attorneys to track and manage their investments and assets holdings to take advantage of all tax benefits permitted by law.

Intangibles

The mechanics of accounting (debiting and crediting appropriate accounts) for these assets are relatively simple, much the same as for any of the above assets. Where the difficulty lies is in their valuation, which is an advanced topic and not something that individual persons and small businesses would likely encounter. For that reason further discussion of items such as patents, copyrights, goodwill, etc. are left out of this Guide.

Chapter 18. Depreciation

This chapter will introduce the concept of depreciation in accounting and give some real life examples for using it.

Basic Concepts

Depreciation is the accounting method for expensing capital purchases over time. There are two reasons that you may want to record depreciation; you are doing bookkeeping for your own personal finances and would like to keep track of your net worth, or you are doing bookkeeping for a small busines and need to produce a financial statement from which you will prepare your tax return.

The method of recording depreciation is the same in either case. but the end goal is different. This section will discuss the differences between the two. But first, some terminology.

- *Accumulated depreciation* - the accumulated total of book depreciation taken over the life of the asset. This is accumulated in the depreciation account in the asset section.

- *Book depreciation* - this is the amount of depreciation that you record in your financial statements per accounting period.

- *Fair market value* - the amount for which an asset could be sold at a given time.

- *Net book value* - this is the difference between the original cost and the depreciation taken to date.

- *Original cost* - this is the amount that the asset cost you to purchase. It includes any cost to get the asset into a condition in which you can use it. For example - shipping, installation costs, special training.

- *Salvage value* - this is the value that you estimate the asset can be sold for at the end of it's useful life (to you).

- *Tax depreciation* - this is the amount of depreciation that you take for income tax purposes.

Personal Finances

Depreciation is used in personal finances to periodically lower an asset's value to give you an accurate estimation of your current net worth. For example, if you owned a car you could keep track of its current value by recording depreciation every year. To accomplish this, you record the original purchase as an asset, and then record a depreciation expense each year (See the section called "Example" for an example). This would result in the net book value being approximately equal to the fair market value of the asset at the end of the year.

Depreciation for personal finance has no tax implications, it is simply used to help you estimate your net worth. Because of this, there are no rules for how you estimate depreciation, use your best judgement.

For which assets should you estimate depreciation? Since the idea of depreciation for personal finances is to give you an estimate of your personal net worth, you need only track depreciation on assets of notable worth that you could potentially sell, such as a car or boat.

Business

As opposed to personal finance where the goal is tracking personal worth, business is concerned with matching the expense of purchasing capital assets with the revenue generated by them. This is done through book depreciation. Businesses must also be concerned with local tax laws covering depreciation of assets. This is known as tax depreciation. The business is free to choose whatever scheme it wants to record book depreciation, but the scheme used for tax depreciation is fixed. More often than not this results in differences between book and tax depreciation, but steps can be taken to reduce these differences.

Now, what purchases should be capitalized? If you expect something that you purchase to help you earn income for more than just the current year, then it should be capitalized. This includes things like land, buildings, equipment, automobiles, and computers - as long as they are used for business purposes. It does not include items that would be considered inventory. So if you made a purchase with the intent to resell the item, it should not be capitalized.

In addition to the purchase of the asset itself, any costs associated with getting the asset into a condition so that you can use it should be capitalized. For example, if you buy a piece of equipment and it needs to be shipped from out of town, and then some electrical work needs to be done so you can plug the machine in, and some specialized training is needed so you know how to use the machine, all these costs would be included in the cost of the equipment.

You also need to know the estimated salvage value of the asset. Generally, this is assumed to be zero. The idea behind knowing the salvage value is that the asset will be depreciated untill the net book value (cost less depreciation) equals the salvage value. Then, when the asset is written off, you will not have a gain or loss resulting from the disposal of the asset.

The last step is to determine the method of depreciation that you want to use. This will be discussed on the next few pages.

Note

Warning: Be aware that different countries can have substantially different tax policies for depreciation; all that this document can really provide is some of the underlying ideas to help you apply your "favorite" tax/depreciation policies.

Estimating Valuation

A central issue with depreciation is to determine how you will estimate the future value of the asset. Compared to the often uncertain estimates one has to do where appreciation of assets is concerned, we are on somewhat firmer ground here. Using sources listed below should make it fairly straight forward to estimate the future value of your depreciating assets.

- *Tax Codes:* For businesses that want to use depreciation for tax purposes, governments tend to set up precise rules as to how you are required to calculate depreciation. Consult your local tax codes, which should explicitly state how to estimate depreciation.

- *Car Blue Book:* For automobiles, it is easy to look up in references such as "Blue Books" estimates of what an automobile should be worth after some period of time in the future. From this you will be able to develop a model of the depreciation.

Depreciation Schemes

A *depreciation scheme* is a mathematical model of how an asset will be expensed over time. For every asset which undergoes depreciation, you will need to decide on a depreciation scheme. An important point to keep in mind is that, for tax purposes, you will need to depreciate your assets at a certain rate. This is called tax depreciation. For financial statement purposes you are free to choose whatever method you want. This is book depreciation. Most small businesses use the same rate for tax and book depreciation. This way there is less of a difference between your net income on the financial statements and your taxable income.

This section will present 3 of the more popular depreciation schemes: *linear*, *geometric*, and *sum of digits*. To simplify the examples, we will assume the salvage value of the asset being depreciated is zero. If you choose to use a salvage value, you would stop depreciating the asset once the net book value equals the salvage value.

1. *Linear depreciation* diminishes the value of an asset by a fixed amount each period until the net value is zero. This is the simplest calculation, as you estimate a useful lifetime, and simply divide the cost equally across that lifetime.

   Example: You have bought a computer for $1500 and wish to depreciate it over a period of 5 years. Each year the amount of depreciation is $300, leading to the following calculations:

Table 18.1. Linear Depreciation Scheme Example

Year	Depreciation	Remaining Value
0	-	1500
1	300	1200
2	300	900
3	300	600
4	300	300
5	300	0

2. *Geometric depreciation* is depreciated by a fixed percentage of the asset value in the previous period. This is a front-weighted depreciation scheme, more depreciation being applied early in the period. In this scheme the value of an asset decreases exponentially leaving a value at the end that is larger than zero (i.e.: a resale value).

   Example: We take the same example as above, with an annual depreciation of 30%.

Table 18.2. Geometric Depreciation Scheme Example

Year	Depreciation	Remaining Value
0	-	1500
1	450	1050
2	315	735
3	220.50	514.50
4	154.35	360.15
5	108.05	252.10

Note

Beware: Tax authorities may require (or allow) a larger percentage in the first period. On the other hand, in Canada, this is reversed, as they permit only a half share of "Capital Cost Allowance" in the first year. The result of this approach is that asset value decreases more rapidly at the beginning than at the end which is probably more realistic for most assets than a linear scheme. This is certainly true for automobiles.

3. *Sum of digits* is a front-weighted depreciation scheme similar to the geometric depreciation, except that the value of the asset reaches zero at the end of the period. This is a front-weighted depreciation

scheme, more depreciation being applied early in the period. This method is most often employed in Anglo/Saxon countries. Here is an illustration:

Example: First you divide the asset value by the sum of the years of use, e.g. for our example from above with an asset worth $1500 that is used over a period of five years you get 1500/(1+2+3+4+5)=100. Depreciation and asset value are then calculated as follows:

Table 18.3. Sum of Digits Depreciation Scheme Example

Year	Depreciation	Remaining Value
0	-	1500
1	100*5=500	1000
2	100*4=400	600
3	100*3=300	300
4	100*2=200	100
5	100*1=100	0

Account Setup

As with most accounting practices, there are a number of different ways to setup depreciation accounts. We will present here a general method which should be flexible enough to handle most situations. The first account you will need is an *Asset Cost* account (GnuCash account type Asset), which is simply a place where you record the original purchase of the asset. Usually this purchase is accomplished by a transaction from your bank account.

In order to keep track of the depreciation of the asset, you will need two depreciation accounts. The first is an *Accumulated Depreciation* account in which to collect the sum of all of the depreciation amounts, and will contain negative values. In GnuCash, this is an account type *asset*. The *Accumulated Depreciation* account is balanced by a *Depreciation Expense* account, in which all periodic depreciation expenses are recorded. In GnuCash, this is an account type *expense*.

Below is a generic account hierarchy for tracking the depreciation of 2 assets, *ITEM1* and *ITEM2*. The *Asset Cost* accounts are balanced by the *Bank* account, the *Accumulated Depreciation* account is balanced by the *Expenses:Depreciation* account.

```
-Assets
  -Fixed Assets
    -ITEM1
      -Cost            (Asset Cost account)
      -Depreciation    (Accumulated Depreciation account)
    -ITEM2
      -Cost            (Asset Cost account)
      -Depreciation    (Accumulated Depreciation account)
  -Current Assets
    -Bank
-Expense
  -Depreciation        (Depreciation Expense account)
```

One of the features of the account hierarchy shown above is that you can readily see some important summary values about your depreciating asset. The *Assets:Fixed Assets:ITEM1* account total shows you the current estimated value for item1, the *Assets:Fixed Assets:ITEM1:Cost* shows you what you originally paid for item1, *Assets:Fixed Assets:ITEM1:Depreciation* shows you your accrued depreciation for item1, and finally, *Expenses:Depreciation* demonstrates the total accrued depreciation of all your assets.

It is certainly possible to use a different account hierarchy. One popular account setup is to combine the *Asset Cost* and *Accrued Depreciation* asset accounts. This has the advantage of having fewer accounts cluttering your account hierarchy, but with the disadvantage that to determine some of the summary details mentioned in the paragraph above you will have to open the account register windows. As with most things, there are many ways to do it, find a way that works best for you.

The actual input of the depreciation amounts is done by hand every accounting period. There is no way in GnuCash (as of yet) to perform the depreciation scheme calculations automatically, or to input the values automatically into the appropriate accounts. However, since an accounting period is typically one year, this really is not much work to do by hand.

Example

Let's go ahead and step through an example. Imagine you are a photographer and you use a car and an expensive camera for your personal business. You will want to track the depreciation on these items, because you can probably deduct the depreciation from your business taxes.

The first step is to build the account hierarchy (as shown in the previous section, replace *ITEM1* and *ITEM2* with "car" and "camera"). Now, record the purchase of your assets by transferring the money from your bank account to the appropriate *Asset Cost* accounts for each item (eg: the *Assets:Fixed Assets:Car:Cost* account for the car). In this example, you start with $30k in the bank, the car cost $20k and the camera cost $10k and were both purchased on January 1, 2000.

The asset depreciation example main window, before depreciation

Looking at the tax codes, we realize that we must report depreciation on these items using the "sum of digits" scheme, over a 5 year period. So, the yearly depreciation amounts for the car come to $6667, $5333, $4000, $2667, $1333 for years 1 to 5 respectively, rounded to the nearest dollar. The yearly depreciation amounts for the camera are $3333, $2667, $2000, $1333, $667. Consult the previous section on Depreciation Schemes for the formula for calculating these values.

For each accounting period (IE: fiscal year) you record the depreciation as an expense in the appropriate *Accrued Depreciation* account (eg: the *Assets:Fixed Assets:Car:Depreciation* account for the car). The two windows below show your car's accrued depreciation account and the main window after the third year (IE: three periods) of depreciation using this sum of digits scheme.

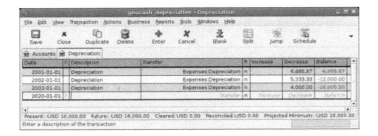

The asset depreciation register window

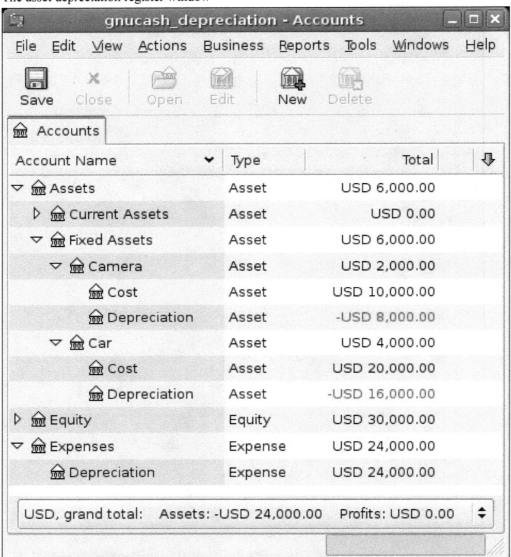

The asset depreciation main window

Note

A Word of Caution: Since depreciation and tax issues are closely related, you may not always be free in choosing your preferred method. Fixing wrong calculations will cost a whole lot more time and trouble than getting the calculations right the first time, so if you plan to depreciate assets, it is wise to make sure of the schemes you will be permitted or required to use.

Chapter 19. Python Bindings

GnuCash historically has always been a traditional application in the sense that you open it, use it to manipulate your financial data via the windows it presents, save your data and close the windows again. This has the inherent limitation that you can only do whatever the windows, menus and toolbars allow you to do.

Sometimes you might need a little more flexibility. For example, you need a report with just a little different information than what the built-in reports provide, or you want to automate a frequently recurring action. Such custom manipulations are ideal candidates to write in one or the other scripting language.

Starting with GnuCash version 2.4 you can write Python scripts to manipulate your financial data.

Note

The Python extensions are an optional feature in the source code. To be able to use Python scripts, GnuCash must have been compiled with this option enabled, otherwise all what follows won't work. At present this option is not enabled by default, so if you need this, you may have to compile GnuCash from source yourself.

The Python extensions come with a couple of ready to use scripts. This chapter will show you how to use some of these.

Note

This chapter is not about how to write your own Python scripts. Refer to the developer documentation for that instead.

Chapter 20. Importing Business Data

Import Bills or Invoices

This functionality is only available by default for versions greater than 2.6

For 2.4.13 the Customers and Vendors importer is an optional module and needs to enabled by editing the file $HOME/.gnucash/config.user, adding the line:

```
(gnc:module-load "gnucash/plugins/bi_import" 0)
```

On Linux systems this file is found at $HOME/.gnucash/config.user and on Mac OSX it is ~/Library/Application Support/Gnucash/config.user. If the file doesn't already exist you will have to create it. After restarting GnuCash, the item will appear at the bottom of the business menu.

In order for the importer to work the data must be in a fixed field length, comma separated line format. A example Python script to convert a downloaded order is shown below.

```python
import sys
import csv


VENDOR_ID="000013"
INFILE=sys.argv[1]
INV_ID=sys.argv[2]
try:
  ACCOUNT=sys.argv[3]
except:
  ACCOUNT="Expenses:Materials General"


Reader = csv.reader(open(INFILE), delimiter=',')

# Need to ignore 1st and last rows

for row in Reader:
  if row[0].isdigit(): # We only use numbered lines
    outline=(INV_ID + ",," + VENDOR_ID + ",,,," + row[1] + " > " + row[4] + ",ea," +
      ACCOUNT + "," + row[2] + "," + row[5].replace("GBP", "") + ",,,,no,,,,,,,")
    print outline
```

Example of a downloaded vendor order from *Rapid Electronics* (UK).

```
line number,product code,quantity,availability,product description,unit price,discounts,line total,delivery,sub total,vat,grand total
1,47-3524,100,100 Available,BC848C SOT-23 NPN TRANSISTOR (INF) (RC),GBP0.03,GBP0.00,GBP0.03
2,47-3278,30,30 Available,L78L05ACZ 0.1A +5V VOLTAGE REG (ST) (RC),GBP0.18,GBP0.00,GBP0.18
3,22-0120,1,1 Available,Tube 34 14pin DIL socket, narrow7.62mm, without central support,GBP1.05,GBP0.00,GBP1.05
4,22-0127,1,0 Available<br />1 on Back Order,Tube 17 28pin DIL socket, wide15.24mm, without central support,GBP1.22,GBP0.00,GBP1.22
5,62-0368,1,1 Available,820R CR25 0.25W CF Resistor Pk 100,GBP0.50,GBP0.00,GBP0.50
6,47-3130,100,100 Available,1N4001 1A 50V SILICON RECTIFIER DIODE RC,GBP0.01,GBP0.00,GBP0.01
7,17-0310,1,1 Available,PROFESSIONAL MINATURE PROBE HOOK RED RC,GBP0.90,GBP0.00,GBP0.90
8,17-0312,1,1 Available,PROFESSIONAL MINATURE PROBE HOOK BLACKRC,GBP0.90,GBP0.00,GBP0.90
```

```
9,34-0655,1,1 Available,PROTOBLOC 2 BREADBOARD,GBP4.39,GBP0.00,GBP4.39
10,18-0200,1,1 Available,PP3 9V ALKALINE BATTERY "Not For Retail Sale",GBP1.37
,,,,,,,,GBP4.95,GBP24.93,GBP4.35,GBP29.28
```

A similar file after processing with the Python script.

```
MEC-0071,,000013,,,,34-0655 > PROTOBLOC 2 BREADBOARD,ea,Expenses:Materials Gen
MEC-0071,,000013,,,,18-0105 > PP3 / PP6 BATTERY CLIP 150MM (RC),ea,Expenses:Ma
MEC-0071,,000013,,,,62-0370 > 1k CR25 0.25W CF Resistor Pk 100,ea,Expenses:Mat
MEC-0071,,000013,,,,62-0354 > 220R CR25 0.25W CF Resistor Pk 100,ea,Expenses:M
MEC-0071,,000013,,,,34-5548 > PLAIN DOCUMENT WALLET ASSORTED PK 50 RE,ea,Exper
MEC-0071,,000013,,,,62-0386 > 4k7 CR25 0.25W CF Resistor Pk 100,ea,Expenses:Ma
MEC-0071,,000013,,,,34-0860 > COPPER CLAD SRBP SS 100 X 160 (RC),ea,Expenses:M
MEC-0071,,000013,,,,18-0163 > PP3 BATTERY HOLDER WITH FLYING LEADS RC,ea,Exper
MEC-0071,,000013,,,,73-4290 > ATMEGA8-16PU 8-BIT MICRO 8K DIL-28 (RC),ea,Exper
MEC-0071,,000013,,,,81-0014 > BC108 NPN GP TRANSISTOR RC,ea,Expenses:Materials
MEC-0071,,000013,,,,DELIVERY,ea,Expenses:Postage,1,4.95,,,,no,,,,,,
MEC-0071,,000013,,,,VAT,tax,Expenses:VAT,1,4.35,,,,no,,,,,,
```

As can be seen there are some fields that are absent and some that are not required for import. The first line is not required and the last line is superfluous as GnuCash will total the order for us. All that is required is to take what we want and produce an output file with the correct format to import into GnuCash. In this case we join the part number and description fields and these become description in GnuCash invoice/bill. We need the qty and part price fields. Contrary to the header line VAT is not included by line and is always zero, the VAT is calculated on the last line as VAT on the order total.

Note

This will cause problems later.
In this example I have assigned the *Expenses:Materials General* account to be the target account. This can be changed after import in the usual way, along with any other data. If there is no such account as *Expenses:Materials General* then that field will be left blank on import and will have to be set manually. Lines beginning with a "#" are regarded as comment lines and ignored.

The script is called with the following command:

python importer.py *file_to_import, invoice_id> file_to_save_as.csv*

This short script can easily be changed to suit any downloaded format. The only restriction is that the final number of field is fixed, at least at the moment. The importer will ignore lines with the wrong number of fields. (This may be fixed in future version). Vendor ID is simply the ID assigned to the specific vendor, or client. The row[N] items refer to the position in the line where the correct data lies. Note that the first field is row[0] NOT row[1].

Once you have converted the file navigate to Business → Invoice & Bill Import to open a new import window. Select the file you have just created, select Bill or Invoice and Comma separated format. At this point the data should show up in the preview window. Check that the field data are in the correct columns before selecting OK. Once imported the invoice can be opened for editing and posting in the usual way.

A note on VAT, or any purchase tax. As previously mentioned *Rapid Electronics* calculate the VAT on the bill total not line by line. GnuCash calculated the VAT per line then totals the VAT. This can lead to inaccuracies in the VAT of the region of a few pennies and is enough to cause problems when reconciling the purchase with your bank or credit card account used to make the purchase. As to how you overcome that, for the moment, is a problem for you to use whatever method suits your conscience or accountant best. Personally I add the VAT as a separate line along with delivery charges manually. So some work is left to the user but the tedium of entering each item eliminated.

Future: Currently the import format is quite strict and many users may have problems with the conversion process. Adding a template for every possible vendor CSV format would be mammoth and likely impossible task notwithstanding the fact the vendors are likely to change the format without informing the GnuCash team. Future import enhancements will be based on user feedback and hopefully the process can be made simpler or more flexible. Note that often "simple" is incompatible with "flexible".

Note

If Python (other languages are avaialble) is not your thing then post a request to *GnuCash user list* [https://lists.gnucash.org/mailman/listinfo/gnucash-user], with an example of your downloaded CSV, and someone may write you a Python script to do the translation.

Notes for Python authors

In order for the import to succeed the number of fields must be adhered to, so the trailing commas are important.

A complete list of the required fields is:

id, date_opened, owner_id, billingid, notes, date, desc, action, account, quantity, price, disc_type, disc_how, discount, taxable, taxincluded, tax_table, date_posted, due_date, account_posted, memo_posted, accu_splits,

Note

Mind the trailing comma.

A brief description of each field

- *id* - The invoice number. All lines must contain this or the line will be rejected.

- *date_opened* - Use the same date format as setup in Preferences. Today's date is inserted if this is blank.

- *owner_id* - ID number of the vendor or customer. All lines must contain this or the line will be rejected.

- *billingid* - Billing ID.

- *notes* - Invoice notes.

- *date* - The date of the item line. Can be left blank for todays date.

- *desc* - Description as per normal invoice or bill.

- *action* - For bills usually "ea".

- *account* - Account to which the item is attributed.

- *quantity* - Quantity of each item. Must contain a value or the line will be rejected.

- *price* - Price of each item. Must contain a value or the line will be rejected.

- *disc_type* - Type of discount, either "%" or "TODO", only applies to invoices. Some experimentation may be required here as may be currency dependent.

- *disc_how* - Only applies to invoices.

- *discount* - Amount of discount to be applied. only applies to invoices.

- *taxable* - Will tax be applied to the item? "yes" or blank.

- *taxincluded* - Is tax included in the item price? "yes" or blank.

- *tax_table* - Tax table to apply to item.

- *date_posted* - If posted, what date. Normally left blank for manual posting after editing the invoice. Use the same date format as setup in Preferences.

- *due_date* - Date payment is due. Use the same date format as setup in Preferences.

- *account_posted* - Posted to what account.

- *memo_posted* - If posted insert memo here.

- *accu_splits* - Accumulate splits? "yes" or blank.

Importing Customers and Vendors

This functionality is only available in the 2.6 versions of GnuCash and is only loaded by default for versions greater than 2.6.

For versions lower than 2.6 the Customers and Vendors importer is an optional module and needs to enabled by editing the file $HOME/.gnucash/config.user, adding the line:

```
(gnc:module-load "gnucash/plugins/customer_import" 0)
```

On Linux systems this file is found at $HOME/.gnucash/config.user and on Mac OSX it is ~/Library/Application Support/Gnucash/config.user. If the file doesn't already exist you will have to create it. After restarting GnuCash the item will appear at the bottom of the business menu.

In order for the importer to work each line in the input file must have the following structure.

```
id, company, name, addr1, addr2, addr3, addr4, phone, fax, email, notes,
shipname, shipaddr1, shipaddr2, shipaddr3, shipaddr4, shiphone, shipfax,
shipmail
```

Fields can be separated with commas or semicolons and each field can be in quotes. These options are selectable in the import dialog. Vendors don't have shipping information so even though the fields have to exist, leave them empty. The id field is optional and if it is empty a new id will be chosen. If the id field has a value this will UPDATE any vendor/customer with the same id. This may not be what you want. Note that in your input file the data must be a single line for each customer/vendor.

The importer does not currently import billing information for customers or vendors, these will have to be edited individually after importing.

Part IV. Appendices

Table of Contents

Appendix A. Migration Guide

This appendix is to help current users of other financial software packages in their migration to GnuCash. We address the conceptual differences between the layout of GnuCash accounts versus other software packages.

Using Accounts vs. Categories

If you are familiar with other personal finance programs, you are already accustomed to tracking your income and expenses as categories. Since GnuCash is a double-entry system (refer to section 2.1), incomes and expenses are tracked in accounts. The basic concept is the same, but the account structure allows more consistency with accepted business practices. So, if you are a business user as well as a home user, GnuCash makes it easy to keep track of your business as well as your personal accounts.

Income and expense accounts give you the same information you would get with categories, but they also give you more flexibility in entering your transactions. In GnuCash, you have the option to enter transactions directly into income and expense accounts through their account registers. Other programs that use categories do not offer this option, because there is no "account register" for a category.

You also have the option in GnuCash to treat income and expense accounts exactly as you would treat categories, if you are more comfortable with that method. In Quicken® and similar programs, transactions require an account and a category. Substitute an income or expense account name in GnuCash where you would normally enter a category name in the other programs, and the result should be the same. We will discuss transaction entry in Chapter 4 in greater detail.

Organization of QIF Files (Discussion)

Common Duplication Issues (Discussion)

Checking QIF Data (Discussion)

Converting XML GnuCash File

The GnuCash XML data file can be transformed to almost any other data format (e.g., QIF, CSV...) quite easily if one is familiar with XSLT. The GnuCash data file is well-formed XML, and it can therefore be run through an XSLT parser with an associated stylesheet. This allows one to transform the file to just about any format that can be designed, given a properly written stylesheet.

A few steps need to be followed. The writing of a stylesheet is a task for a different time, but if you can get one written, here's what you need to do:

1. Copy the GnuCash XML data file to a working file.

   ### Note

   If the file was last modified by a version of GnuCash older than 2.0, then before to continue to the next step you will need to modify the working file's <gnc-v2> tag to read something like this:

```
<gnc-v2 xmlns:cd="http://www.gnucash.org/XML/cd"
        xmlns:book="http://www.gnucash.org/XML/book"
        xmlns:gnc="http://www.gnucash.org/XML/gnc"
        xmlns:cmdty="http://www.gnucash.org/XML/cmdty"
        xmlns:trn="http://www.gnucash.org/XML/trn"
        xmlns:split="http://www.gnucash.org/XML/split"
        xmlns:act="http://www.gnucash.org/XML/act"
        xmlns:price="http://www.gnucash.org/XML/price"
        xmlns:ts="http://www.gnucash.org/XML/ts"
        xmlns:slot="http://www.gnucash.org/XML/kvpslot"
        xmlns:cust="http://www.gnucash.org/XML/cust"
        xmlns:entry="http://www.gnucash.org/XML/entry"
        xmlns:lot="http://www.gnucash.org/XML/lot"
        xmlns:invoice="http://www.gnucash.org/XML/invoice"
        xmlns:owner="http://www.gnucash.org/XML/owner"
        xmlns:job="http://www.gnucash.org/XML/job"
        xmlns:billterm="http://www.gnucash.org/XML/billterm"
        xmlns:bt-days="http://www.gnucash.org/XML/bt-days"
        xmlns:sx="http://www.gnucash.org/XML/sx"
        xmlns:fs="http://www.gnucash.org/XML/fs"
        xmlns:addr="http://www.gnucash.org/XML/custaddr">
```

You can put pretty much anything you want behind the equal signs, but a URL is what is typically used.

2. Create an XSLT stylesheet containing the transformation your desire, or obtain one that's already written (AFAIK, there aren't any, but I'm working on a CSV one).

3. Install an XSLT processor such as Saxon (http://saxon.sourceforge.net/) or Xalan-J (http://xml.apache.org/). Any conforming processor will do, really...

4. Run the work file and the stylesheet through the processor according to the processor's instructions.

5. You will now have a file in the desired output format. An enterprising individual could go so far as to write a stylesheet to transform the GnuCash data file to an OpenOffice spreadsheet (or vice-versa, for that matter). Such things as QIF ought to be a little less work.

Benefits are that you don't need to write a Scheme module or a new C routine to do this transformation. Anyone who knows or can learn XML and XSLT can perform this task. Not much harder, really, than writing a Web page....

Anyhow, I just wanted this tidbit to be captured somewhere permanently. The process works on 2.6.8 datafiles, and ought to work on earlier versions, too.

Appendix B. Frequently Asked Questions

This is a list of questions asked on the mailing lists for which there really is no section in the documentation covering the subject.

Sources of Information

Q: Where's the FAQ?

A: You're looking at it. The most up-to-date copy can be found within the GnuCash Wiki [http://wiki.gnucash.org/wiki/FAQ].

Q: Are there mailing lists for GnuCash?

A: Yes. Go to http://lists.gnucash.org/mailman/listinfo/gnucash-user and http://lists.gnucash.org/mailman/listinfo/gnucash-devel to subscibe.

Q: Is there a searchable archive for the mailing lists?

A: Yes, you can search the mail list archives at http://news.gmane.org/gmane.comp.gnome.apps.gnucash.devel and http://news.gmane.org/gmane.comp.gnome.apps.gnucash.user (and http://news.gmane.org/gmane.comp.gnome.apps.gnucash.german if you speak German).

Q: Are there other means of obtaining support for GnuCash?

A: Yes. Many of the developers hang out on icq in the #gnucash discussion on irc.gnome.org. Also, there is a wiki online at http://wiki.gnucash.org/wiki/GnuCash.

General Information

Q: Can I run GnuCash on Windows?

A: Yes. Starting with release 2.2.0, GnuCash is also available on Windows.

Other related options would be colinux, VMWare and a windows-based X-server hosting a remote GnuCash session.

Q: I heard it is too hard to compile GnuCash!

A: This was probably true at the time when 1.6.0 was released. It is no longer true today, as almost every distribution ships with all the necessary libraries (except g-wrap, which means there is in fact "one" extra library to be installed before compiling GnuCash). However, by default, distributions won't install the development packages of the required libraries, so you might need to start your distribution's installer program and tell it to install not only the library packages but also the -devel packages. In general, it was noted that this problem concerns many applications in the gnome domain, and this also boils down to the fact that there is no such thing as "one monolithic gnome package".

Q: Is there a batch mode (non-interactive) available for GnuCash, for building reports, etc?

A: No, for now GnuCash must be run interactively.

Q: Can multiple people access the same datafile in GnuCash?

A: You can have multiple people with access to the same datafile, but they cannot use the data file simultaneously.

To setup multi-person access, all the people must have read/write access to the directory containing the file (to read the other's created files, and to create new files). One way to do this is by creating a user group and setting the data directory to be owned by the shared group and set to mode 2775. The "2" makes the directory setgid which copies the permissions to all files.

Q: Why is GnuCash written in C?

A: The core functionality of GnuCash is written in C, but do not forget that much of this can be accessed through Guile (scheme). There are a number of reasons for why GnuCash is written in C. The first is historical, GnuCash was started in 1996 (or maybe even earlier!) and many of the OOP (C++, Java, Python) compilers were not yet mature and standarized enough on the variety of platforms considered at that time, so C was the only option at that time. A second reason is because the standard GUI GnuCash uses is GTK, which is written in C.

Q: Why don't you rewrite GnuCash in programming language xyz so that I can contribute easily?

A: The quick answer is "We won't". The longer answer is complex but still amounts to "We won't". GnuCash is a large body of code maintained by a small group of developers who are comfortable in C and Scheme (Guile). Actually, 80% of it is in C and approx. 13% is in Scheme/Lisp. There is no valid reason that would justify rewriting this amount of existing code in a newer language. Also, creating language bindings to recent languages such as Python or Ruby or (insert your favourite language here) is labor intensive, and we're already stretched pretty thin maintaining and developing the existing code.

Having said that, this is an open source project and you're free to do with it or contribute what you want. Just don't expect much support if the reason for your changes is that you're not willing to learn C or Scheme. Also, GnuCash used to have SWIG bindings (http://www.swig.org) which have been used for some perl programming code. According to a list discussion, these SWIG bindings might still be a way to include other languages into GnuCash, but currently they are unused and unmaintained.

Q: I really want feature XYZ but GnuCash doesn't have it. How do I get it added?

A: Ask nicely. :-) You can file an enhancement request at http://bugzilla.gnome.org/enter_bug.cgi? product=GnuCash. Please bear in mind to describe your proposed enhancement as verbosely as possible. The trick here is to learn how to give the best information to the programmers about what your proposed new feature should do. If you want to speed up development significantly, consider donating some money as described on GnuCashDevelopment.

Q: Is there a web interface available for GnuCash?

A: No

Q: How can I provide security for GnuCash data using CFS, etc.)

A: Unanswered

Q: How can I contribute to the GnuCash project?

A: We're working on a more formal process, but for now you should subscribe to the mailing list at http://lists.gnucash.org/mailman/listinfo/gnucash-user and http://lists.gnucash.org/mailman/listinfo/gnucash-devel and discuss what you can contribute with the participants on the lists. Please be aware that GnuCash is a large body of code written in C and Scheme (see the FAQ above, "Why is GnuCash written in C?" if you want to know why). If these are languages that you are not willing to work with, consider contributing in other ways.

Q: I think I found a bug. How do I report it?

A: First of all, try to verify that it is indeed a bug and that it has not been reported before. Search the mail list archives (see FAQ above). Then search the Gnome Bugzilla [http://bugzilla.gnome.org] database.

If you feel you have indeed found a bug, you can then report it at http://bugzilla.gnome.org/enter_bug.cgi?product=GnuCash. Please bear in mind to report your bug as verbosely as possible. The trick here is to learn how to give the best information to the programmers about how to reproduce bugs. A Programmer will usually only be able to fix a bug they can see, if you can't make the programmer see your bug, it won't get fixed!

Using GnuCash

Q: How can I move the transactions from account "A" into account "B", thus combining them?

A: At present, GnuCash does not offer a way to move groups of splits from one account to another. You will need to move them one at a time. Open the register for account "A" and select the pulldown menu item View → Transaction Journal to expose all the splits. For every split where the "Account" field shows account "A" reset it to account "B". To do this quickly and safely, first use **Ctrl+C** to copy the destination account name ("account B") to the clipboard. Then highlight each reference to account "A" by double clicking on it and use **Ctrl+V** to paste the destination account name. Pressing **Enter** after each paste, silently moves the transaction out of the register.

Be careful! If you inadvertently set the "Account" field to an unintended location, you will need to search through all your accounts to find the lost transaction to correct your mistake.

Q: Is it possible to merge two GnuCash files?

A: At present this is not possible.

Q: How can I save a template of my account structure?

A: This is available from the menu: File → Export → Export Accounts

Q: When I search for customers (or anything else for that matter), how can I return a list of everything?

A: Enter a search criteria of matches regex, and place a single dot "." in the text field area. Then, click Find. The regular expression "." means to match anything.

Q: How can I record a transaction on different dates (actual date and bank date)?

A: You record the transaction on the date you write the check or initiate the transaction. When it "clears" the bank, you can click in the "Reconciled" field to "clear" the transaction (change the "n"on-reconciled to "c"leared).

Accounting

Q: How do I treat taxes? As an account payable or as an expense?

A: This is a loaded question, and you should really talk to your accountant. How you treat taxes really depends on what kind of taxes they are, and how you WANT to treat them.. In some cases they are expenses, in some cases they are liabilities.

Appendix C. Contributed Account Trees

UK Vat

Account types (only shown if different to parent type)

- [E] Expense

- [I] Income

- [A] Asset

- [L] Liability

- [Q] Equity

- [B] Bank accounts

- [C] Credit Cards

- [R] Accounts Receivable

- [P] Accounts Payable

(Box n) refers to VAT form box number (I actually have these as descriptions to the account to remind me)

Add all the (Box n -part) together to get the whole (Box n) The VAT shows you liability - if its negative they owe you.

Capital Equipment (Box 7 - part) and (Box 6 - part) is the value of all *additions* (purchases) made over the VAT return period - not the absolute value, nor the difference in value unless that difference is wholly due to new purchases. Depreciation, losses (e.g a write off of faulty item) and other reductions in capital value are not included. If you sell a capital item then that sale and its VAT is recorded under Income. The asset is "converted to cash", so the "net of VAT" increase in your bank account, when the invoice is payed, is matched by a decrease in capital.


```
Bank Accounts [B]
|___ Main Account
|___ Reserve Account
```

```
Cash [A]
```

```
Assets [A]
|___ Capital Equipment   (Box 7 - Part) - additions only, not absolute value
|      |___ Computers     Can be depreciated to zero this year
|      |___ EEC reverse VAT purchase  (Box 6 - Part) create sub-accounts if needed
|___ Other
```

Receivable [R] Customers to whom you give credit - (business section)

Cards [C]
|___ Card 1

Liabilities [L]
|___ Owed Corp Tax
|___ Owed Fees
|___ Owed Tax / NI
|___ Other

VAT [L]   Net (Box 5)
|___ i/p [A]   purchases (Box4)
|___ o/p [L]   (Box3)
        |___EEC   on reverse VAT purchases (Box 2)
        |___Sales   all including zero rate UK/ EEC and World (Box1)

Payable [P]   Suppliers who give you credit (business section)

Equity [Q]
|___ Corp Tax
|___ Director's Loan
|___ Dividends
| |___   Director1
| |___   Director2
| |___   Shareholder 1
|___ Grants (and stuff that does not count as income)
|___Opening Balances

Income [I]   (Box 6 - part)
|___ Interest
|___ Misc
|___ Sales
        |___   EEC
| |____ goods (Box 8) (sub accounts as needed)
| |____ services includes software (sub accounts as needed)
| |___ UK
|____ World

Expenses [E]
|__Depreciation
|__ Emoluments
| |___   Directors Fees
| |___   NI Employer
| |___   Employee 1
| | |___NI
| | |___Net Salary
| | |___Stakeholder
| | |___Tax
|___ Other Non VAT Expenses
|___ VAT Purchases   (Box 7 - part)
        |___   Accountancy
        |___   Bank Charges
        |___   Consumables
        |___   EEC reverse VAT purchases (Box 6 - Part)

```
|       |___ goods (Box 9) (sub accounts as needed)
|       |___ services   includes software (sub accounts as needed)
|___ Office
|___ Phone and Internet
|___ Software
|___ Subscriptions
|___ Sundry
|___ Travel / Accom
```

Appendix D. Auxiliary File Formats

These are the formats of some auxiliary files used by GnuCash.

Check Format Files (*.chk)

Overview

The check format file is used to tell GnuCash how to print a check or checks onto a page of paper. This file first describes the overall layout of a page (number of checks, orientation, etc) and then describes the layout of the specific items on a single check. The file is organized as a typical Key/Value file used by many Linux applications. Keys/values pairs are grouped into sections that begin with the group name enclosed in square brackets.

GnuCash looks for check format files in two different locations when you bring up the check printing dialog. The first location is typically /usr/share/gnucash/checks, where check files distributed with the application can be found. The second location is the user private ~/.gnucash/checks directory. Users may add check formats at any time (even while GnuCash is running) simply by dropping a new *.chk file in this directory. The next time the check printing dialog is opened the new check format will appear in the list of available check formats.

Note

Printing functions differently depending on the version of GTK that is installed on your system. When GnuCash is using a version of GTK prior to 2.10 all offsets are measured from the lower left corner of the page or check. When using GTK 2.10 or later, all offsets are measured from the upper left corner of the page or check.

Example file

A typical GnuCash check file is presented below. The contents of this file will be described in the next sections.

```
[Top]
Guid = 67b144d1-96a5-48d5-9337-0e1083bbf229
Title = Quicken/QuickBooks (tm) US-Letter
Rotation = 0.0
Translation = 0.0;4.0
Show_Grid = false
Show_Boxes = false

[Check Positions]
Height = 252.0
Names = Top;Middle;Bottom

[Check Items]
Type_1 = PAYEE
Coords_1 = 90.0;102.0;400.0;20.0

Type_2 = AMOUNT_WORDS
Coords_2 = 90.0;132.0
```

```
Type_3 = AMOUNT_NUMBER
Blocking_Chars_3 = true
Coords_3 = 500.0;102.0

Type_4 = DATE
Coords_4 = 500.0;67.0

Type_5 = NOTES
Coords_5 = 50.0;212.0
```

Field Descriptions

Top Group

This section of the check file describes the overall layout of a page of checks (or check) that goes into the printer.

Table D.1. Overall Page Description Fields

Name	Type	Required	Description
Guid	string	mandatory	The guid is used to uniquely identify a check format to GnuCash. It must be unique across the entire set of application supplied and user supplied check formats. If you copy an application check file as the basis of your own check format, you must change this value. The *uuidgen* program may be used to generate these identifiers.
Title	string	mandatory	The title is used to uniquely identify a check format to the user. This value is presented verbatim in the check format list of the check printing dialog. If you copy an application check file as the basis of your own check format, you should change this value. The title may be any utf-8 string.
Font	string	optional	If supplied, this is the default font used to print all text items on this

Name	Type	Required	Description
			check. This field can contain any string that is acceptable by gtk as a font specifier. If this field is omitted, the default font is the font specified in the GnuCash preferences dialog. A typical string would be "sans 12".
Blocking_Chars	boolean	optional	If supplied, this is the default used when printing all *TEXT* items on this check. When set to true, will print *** before and after each text field on the check. Blocking characters are printed to protect check fields from alteration. For example, the amount field may be printed as ***100.00***
DateFormat	boolean	optional	If supplied, this is the default used when printing all *DATE* items on this check. When set to true, will print the format of the DATE in 8 point type, centered and below the actual DATE. For example DDMMYYYY.
Rotation	double	optional	This value specified the rotation of the entire page (in degrees) around the origin point. For gtk versions prior to 2.10, the origin point is in the lower left corner of the page and rotation values increase in the counter-clockwise direction. For gtk version 2.10 and later, the origin point is in the upper left corner of the page and rotation values increase in the clockwise direction. Rotation of the

Name	Type	Required	Description
			page is applied before translation.
Translation	list of 2 doubles	optional	These values specify the x and y translation of the entire page (in points) relative to the origin point. For gtk versions prior to 2.10, the origin point is in the lower left corner of the page and translation values increase moving up and to the right. For gtk version 2.10 and later, the origin point is in the upper left corner of the page and translation values increase moving down and to the right. Rotation of the page is applied before translation.
Show_Grid	boolean	optional	If this value is set to *true* then GnuCash will draw a grid on the page, starting at the origin with the lines spaced every 50 points. This can be helpful when creating a check format file.
Show_Boxes	boolean	optional	If this value is set to *true* then for each item where the width and height have been specified, GnuCash will draw a box showing location and maximum size of that item . This can be helpful when creating a check format file.

Note

The Blocking_Chars and DateFormat options are defined for all check formats in Edit->Preferences->Printing. It is recommened that these global options be set to false (the default), and that the options be set for individual Check Items as described below.

Check Positions Group

This group of items specifies how multiple checks are laid out on the same sheet of paper, and gives names to each of these check locations so that a user can specify which check location that GnuCash should print.

This entire group of key/value pairs is optional, and should be omitted if the format file only specifies a single check per page of paper.

Table D.2. Multiple Checks Per Page Fields

Name	Type	Required	Description
Height	double	mandatory	This field specifies the height of a single check on the page. If there are multiple checks per page then this item is mandatory. If there is only a single check per page, this entire section should be omitted.
Names	list of strings	mandatory	This field specifies the names of the check locations that can be printed on each page. These names represent the check positions starting from the top of the page and moving downward. The names are presented verbatim in the check position list of the check printing dialog. A typical value for this field is "Top;Middle;Bottom", but it could also be "First;Second;Third" or any other set of strings that clearly identify the check locations. If there are multiple checks per page then this item is mandatory. If there is only a single check per page, this entire section should be omitted.

Check Items Group

This section specifies the individual items that are printed on the check. There is no limit to the number of items that may be present in this section, and any given type of item can be repeated multiple times. This allows for the printing of checks that have a side stub, or for the one-per-page business checks that have both the check and multiple check stubs on the same page. For example, to print the payee name on a business check and on both stubs, simply specify three payee items with differing print coordinates.

Each key names in this section explicitly includes the item number to which it applies. E.G. The key named Type_1 applies to the first item to be printed, and the key Coords_3 applies to the third item to be printed. Item numbers start at one and increase sequentially. Any gap in the numbering sequence is interpreted by

GnuCash as the end of the item list. Items are printed in the order of their item numbers, not in the order in which they appear in the file.

Each item specified must include a type declaration. The rest of the parameters for that item depend upon the particular type of that item. See Table D.4, "Individual Check Item Types" for a list of valid item types and their required parameters.

Table D.3. Individual Check Item Fields

Name	Type	Required	Description
Type_*n*	string	mandatory	This field specifies the type of a single item to be printed on a check. See Table D.4, "Individual Check Item Types" for a list of valid item types.
Coords_*n*	list of 2 or 4 doubles	mandatory	This field specifies the coordinates where the item should be placed on a check, and optionally also specifies the width and height of the item. The numbers in order are the X and Y offset of the lower left corner of the item, and optionally the width and height of the item. If the width is supplied then the height must also be supplied, so this field will always contain two or four numbers. For gtk versions prior to 2.10, the origin point is in the lower left corner of the page and translation values increase moving up and to the right. For gtk version 2.10 and later, the origin point is in the upper left corner of the page and translation values increase moving down and to the right. **Note** Regardless of whether the origin is at the top or the bottom

Name	Type	Required	Description
			of the page, the coordinates always specify the lower left point of the item.
Font_*n*	string	optional	If supplied, this is the font used to print this specific text item. This field can contain any string that is acceptable by gtk as a font specifier. If this field is omitted, the default font is the font specified in the *Top* section of the check description file, or if that was omitted the font specified in the GnuCash preferences dialog. This field is only recognized when using gtk version 2.10 or later.
Align_*n*	string	optional	If supplied, this is the alignment used to print this specific text item. This field must contain one of the strings "left", "center" or "right". If this field is omitted, the text will be left aligned. This field is only recognized when using gtk version 2.10 or later.
Text_*n*	string	optional	This field is only used when the item type is *TEXT*. It specifies the utf-8 text that should be printed on the check.
Filename_*n*	string	optional	This field is only used when the item type is *PICTURE*. It specifies the filename of the image that should be printed on the check. The string may specify either an absolute path name or as a relative path name. If a relative path name is specified, GnuCash first looks in in the

Name	Type	Required	Description
			application check format folder (typically `/usr/share/gnucash/checks`) for the image file, and if it isn't found there then it looks in the user private `~/.gnucash/checks` directory for the image. This field is only recognized when using gtk version 2.10 or later.
Blocking_Chars_*n*	boolean	optional	If supplied, this will set the print *Blocking_Chars* option for this item.
DateFormat_*n*	boolean	optional	If supplied, this will set the print *DateFormat* option for this item.

These are the individual items that can be printed on a check. All items require the coordinates on the page where the item should be printed. The majority of these items result in text being printed on the page, and these items may have individual font and alignments specified. For example, the numerical amount of a check could be printed right justified while everything else is printed left justified. Other types may have unique parameters.

Table D.4. Individual Check Item Types

Name	Required Fields	Optional Fields	Description
PAYEE	Coords	Font Align Blocking_Chars	This type value tells GnuCash to print the check payee name at the specified coordinates.
DATE	Coords	Font Align Blocking_Chars DateFormat	This type value tells GnuCash to print the check date at the specified coordinates.
NOTES	Coords	Font Align Blocking_Chars	This type value tells GnuCash to print the transaction notes field at the specified coordinates.
CHECK_NUMBER	Coords	Font Align Blocking_Chars	This type value tells GnuCash to print the check number at the specified coordinates. The check number reflects the book option selection under File → Properties

Name	Required Fields	Optional Fields	Description
			for number source (transaction number or anchor-split action - see Use Split Action Field for Number [ghelp:gnucash-help?num-action-book-option] in the Book Options section of the GnuCash Help Manual).
MEMO	Coords	Font Align Blocking_Chars	This type value tells GnuCash to print the split memo field at the specified coordinates.
ACTION	Coords	Font Align Blocking_Chars	This type value tells GnuCash to print the split action field at the specified coordinates. However, the printed field reflects the book option selection under File → Properties for number source (transaction number or anchor-split action - see Use Split Action Field for Number [ghelp:gnucash-help?num-action-book-option] in the Book Options section of the GnuCash Help Manual). If number source for the book is specified as anchor-split action, this field will instead print the transaction number field.
AMOUNT_WORDS	Coords	Font Align Blocking_Chars	This type value tells GnuCash to print the check amount in words at the specified coordinates. The amount will appear similar to the string "One thousand, two hundred thirty four and 56/100".
AMOUNT_NUMBER	Coords	Font Align Blocking_Chars	This type value tells GnuCash to print the check amount in numbers at the specified coordinates. The amount

Name	Required Fields	Optional Fields	Description
			will appear similar to the number "$1,234.56".
ADDRESS	Coords	Font Align Blocking_Chars	This type value tells GnuCash to print the address at the specified coordinates.
SPLITS_ACCOUNT	Coords	Font Align Blocking_Chars	This type value tells GnuCash to print the account names for each split entry stating at the specified coordinates. See the note on splits printing.
SPLITS_AMOUNT	Coords	Font Align Blocking_Chars	This type value tells GnuCash to print the amount for each split entry stating at the specified coordinates. Amounts are printed with currency symbols. See the note on splits printing.
SPLITS_MEMO	Coords	Font Align Blocking_Chars	This type value tells GnuCash to print the memo text for each split entry stating at the specified coordinates. See the note on splits printing.
TEXT	Coords, Text	Font Align Blocking_Chars	This type value tells GnuCash to print an arbitrary string at the specified coordinates. The string to be printed is specified with the *Text_n* key.
PICTURE	Coords, Filename	(none)	This type value tells GnuCash to print an image at the specified coordinates. The image to be printed is specified with the *Filename_n* key. This type is only recognized when using gtk version 2.10 or later.

Note

SPLIT items include all split entries for the transaction except for the split that applies to the current account register (referred to as the anchor-split). This is usually the last split listed when splits are displayed in the register. The coordinate location defines the lower left location for the split information.

Creating Check Format Files

Creating your own check format file is a fairly simple task. The easiest way to start is to copy an existing check format file from the application directory (typically `/usr/share/gnucash/checks`) to the directory `~/.gnucash/checks`. Make sure to change the guid so the new file will be accepted by gnucash, and change the title to something descriptive. Then change or add individual item fields as necessary. You can also create a new check file by clicking the Save Format button on the Custom format page of the check printing dialog.

Note

Key names are case sensitive. If you're having problems with a check format file, ensure that all key names have capital letters as documented above.

Appendix E. GNU Free Documentation License

Version 1.1, March 2000
Copyright © 2000 Free Software Foundation, Inc.

Free Software Foundation, Inc. 59 Temple Place,
  Suite 330, Boston, MA
  02111-1307 USA

Everyone is permitted to copy and distribute verbatim copies of this license document, but changing it is not allowed.

0. PREAMBLE

The purpose of this License is to make a manual, textbook, or other written document "free" in the sense of freedom: to assure everyone the effective freedom to copy and redistribute it, with or without modifying it, either commercially or noncommercially. Secondarily, this License preserves for the author and publisher a way to get credit for their work, while not being considered responsible for modifications made by others.

This License is a kind of "copyleft", which means that derivative works of the document must themselves be free in the same sense. It complements the GNU General Public License, which is a copyleft license designed for free software.

We have designed this License in order to use it for manuals for free software, because free software needs free documentation: a free program should come with manuals providing the same freedoms that the software does. But this License is not limited to software manuals; it can be used for any textual work, regardless of subject matter or whether it is published as a printed book. We recommend this License principally for works whose purpose is instruction or reference.

1. APPLICABILITY AND DEFINITIONS

This License applies to any manual or other work that contains a notice placed by the copyright holder saying it can be distributed under the terms of this License. The "Document", below, refers to any such manual or work. Any member of the public is a licensee, and is addressed as "you".

A "Modified Version" of the Document means any work containing the Document or a portion of it, either copied verbatim, or with modifications and/or translated into another language.

A "Secondary Section" is a named appendix or a front-matter section of the Document [238] that deals exclusively with the relationship of the publishers or authors of the Document to the Document's overall subject (or to related matters) and contains nothing that could fall directly within that overall subject. (For example, if the Document is in part a textbook of mathematics, a Secondary Section may not explain any mathematics.) The relationship could be a matter of historical connection with the subject or with related matters, or of legal, commercial, philosophical, ethical or political position regarding them.

The "Invariant Sections" are certain Secondary Sections [238] whose titles are designated, as being those of Invariant Sections, in the notice that says that the Document [238] is released under this License.

The "Cover Texts" are certain short passages of text that are listed, as Front-Cover Texts or Back-Cover Texts, in the notice that says that the Document [238] is released under this License.

A "Transparent" copy of the Document [238] means a machine-readable copy, represented in a format whose specification is available to the general public, whose contents can be viewed and edited directly and straightforwardly with generic text editors or (for images composed of pixels) generic paint programs or (for drawings) some widely available drawing editor, and that is suitable for input to text formatters or for automatic translation to a variety of formats suitable for input to text formatters. A copy made in an otherwise Transparent file format whose markup has been designed to thwart or discourage subsequent modification by readers is not Transparent. A copy that is not "Transparent" is called "Opaque".

Examples of suitable formats for Transparent copies include plain ASCII without markup, Texinfo input format, LaTeX input format, SGML or XML using a publicly available DTD, and standard-conforming simple HTML designed for human modification. Opaque formats include PostScript, PDF, proprietary formats that can be read and edited only by proprietary word processors, SGML or XML for which the DTD and/or processing tools are not generally available, and the machine-generated HTML produced by some word processors for output purposes only.

The "Title Page" means, for a printed book, the title page itself, plus such following pages as are needed to hold, legibly, the material this License requires to appear in the title page. For works in formats which do not have any title page as such, "Title Page" means the text near the most prominent appearance of the work's title, preceding the beginning of the body of the text.

2. VERBATIM COPYING

You may copy and distribute the Document [238] in any medium, either commercially or noncommercially, provided that this License, the copyright notices, and the license notice saying this License applies to the Document are reproduced in all copies, and that you add no other conditions whatsoever to those of this License. You may not use technical measures to obstruct or control the reading or further copying of the copies you make or distribute. However, you may accept compensation in exchange for copies. If you distribute a large enough number of copies you must also follow the conditions in section 3.

You may also lend copies, under the same conditions stated above, and you may publicly display copies.

3. COPYING IN QUANTITY

If you publish printed copies of the Document [238] numbering more than 100, and the Document's license notice requires Cover Texts [238], you must enclose the copies in covers that carry, clearly and legibly, all these Cover Texts: Front-Cover Texts on the front cover, and Back-Cover Texts on the back cover. Both covers must also clearly and legibly identify you as the publisher of these copies. The front cover must present the full title with all words of the title equally prominent and visible. You may add other material on the covers in addition. Copying with changes limited to the covers, as long as they preserve the title of the Document [238] and satisfy these conditions, can be treated as verbatim copying in other respects.

If the required texts for either cover are too voluminous to fit legibly, you should put the first ones listed (as many as fit reasonably) on the actual cover, and continue the rest onto adjacent pages.

If you publish or distribute Opaque [238] copies of the Document [238] numbering more than 100, you must either include a machine-readable Transparent [238] copy along with each Opaque copy, or state in or with each Opaque copy a publicly-accessible computer-network location containing a complete Transparent copy of the Document, free of added material, which the general network-using public has access to download anonymously at no charge using public-standard network protocols. If you use the latter option, you must take reasonably prudent steps, when you begin distribution of Opaque copies in quantity, to ensure that this Transparent copy will remain thus accessible at the stated location until at least one year after the last time you distribute an Opaque copy (directly or through your agents or retailers) of that edition to the public.

It is requested, but not required, that you contact the authors of the Document [238] well before redistributing any large number of copies, to give them a chance to provide you with an updated version of the Document.

4. MODIFICATIONS

You may copy and distribute a Modified Version [238] of the Document [238] under the conditions of sections 2 and 3 above, provided that you release the Modified Version under precisely this License, with the Modified Version filling the role of the Document, thus licensing distribution and modification of the Modified Version to whoever possesses a copy of it. In addition, you must do these things in the Modified Version:

- **A.** Use in the Title Page [239] (and on the covers, if any) a title distinct from that of the Document [238], and from those of previous versions (which should, if there were any, be listed in the History section of the Document). You may use the same title as a previous version if the original publisher of that version gives permission.

- **B.** List on the Title Page [239], as authors, one or more persons or entities responsible for authorship of the modifications in the Modified Version [238], together with at least five of the principal authors of the Document [238] (all of its principal authors, if it has less than five).

- **C.** State on the Title Page [239] the name of the publisher of the Modified Version [238], as the publisher.

- **D.** Preserve all the copyright notices of the Document [238].

- **E.** Add an appropriate copyright notice for your modifications adjacent to the other copyright notices.

- **F.** Include, immediately after the copyright notices, a license notice giving the public permission to use the Modified Version [238] under the terms of this License, in the form shown in the Addendum below.

- **G.** Preserve in that license notice the full lists of Invariant Sections [238] and required Cover Texts [238] given in the Document's [238] license notice.

- **H.** Include an unaltered copy of this License.

- **I.** Preserve the section entitled "History", and its title, and add to it an item stating at least the title, year, new authors, and publisher of the Modified Version [238]as given on the Title Page [239]. If there is no section entitled "History" in the Document [238], create one stating the title, year, authors, and publisher of the Document as given on its Title Page, then add an item describing the Modified Version as stated in the previous sentence.

- **J.** Preserve the network location, if any, given in the Document [238] for public access to a Transparent [238] copy of the Document, and likewise the network locations given in the Document for previous versions it was based on. These may be placed in the "History" section. You may omit a network location for a work that was published at least four years before the Document itself, or if the original publisher of the version it refers to gives permission.

- **K.** In any section entitled "Acknowledgements" or "Dedications", preserve the section's title, and preserve in the section all the substance and tone of each of the contributor acknowledgements and/or dedications given therein.

- **L.** Preserve all the Invariant Sections [238] of the Document [238], unaltered in their text and in their titles. Section numbers or the equivalent are not considered part of the section titles.

- **M.**   Delete any section entitled "Endorsements". Such a section may not be included in the Modified Version [238].

- **N.**   Do not retitle any existing section as "Endorsements" or to conflict in title with any Invariant Section [238].

If the Modified Version [238] includes new front-matter sections or appendices that qualify as Secondary Sections [238] and contain no material copied from the Document, you may at your option designate some or all of these sections as invariant. To do this, add their titles to the list of Invariant Sections [238] in the Modified Version's license notice. These titles must be distinct from any other section titles.

You may add a section entitled "Endorsements", provided it contains nothing but endorsements of your Modified Version [238] by various parties--for example, statements of peer review or that the text has been approved by an organization as the authoritative definition of a standard.

You may add a passage of up to five words as a Front-Cover Text [238], and a passage of up to 25 words as a Back-Cover Text [238], to the end of the list of Cover Texts [238] in the Modified Version [238]. Only one passage of Front-Cover Text and one of Back-Cover Text may be added by (or through arrangements made by) any one entity. If the Document [238] already includes a cover text for the same cover, previously added by you or by arrangement made by the same entity you are acting on behalf of, you may not add another; but you may replace the old one, on explicit permission from the previous publisher that added the old one.

The author(s) and publisher(s) of the Document [238] do not by this License give permission to use their names for publicity for or to assert or imply endorsement of any Modified Version [238].

5. COMBINING DOCUMENTS

You may combine the Document [238] with other documents released under this License, under the terms defined in section 4 above for modified versions, provided that you include in the combination all of the Invariant Sections [238] of all of the original documents, unmodified, and list them all as Invariant Sections of your combined work in its license notice.

The combined work need only contain one copy of this License, and multiple identical Invariant Sections [238] may be replaced with a single copy. If there are multiple Invariant Sections with the same name but different contents, make the title of each such section unique by adding at the end of it, in parentheses, the name of the original author or publisher of that section if known, or else a unique number. Make the same adjustment to the section titles in the list of Invariant Sections in the license notice of the combined work.

In the combination, you must combine any sections entitled "History" in the various original documents, forming one section entitled "History"; likewise combine any sections entitled "Acknowledgements", and any sections entitled "Dedications". You must delete all sections entitled "Endorsements."

6. COLLECTIONS OF DOCUMENTS

You may make a collection consisting of the Document [238] and other documents released under this License, and replace the individual copies of this License in the various documents with a single copy that is included in the collection, provided that you follow the rules of this License for verbatim copying of each of the documents in all other respects.

You may extract a single document from such a collection, and dispbibute it individually under this License, provided you insert a copy of this License into the extracted document, and follow this License in all other respects regarding verbatim copying of that document.

7. AGGREGATION WITH INDEPENDENT WORKS

A compilation of the Document [238] or its derivatives with other separate and independent documents or works, in or on a volume of a storage or distribution medium, does not as a whole count as a Modified Version [238] of the Document, provided no compilation copyright is claimed for the compilation. Such a compilation is called an "aggregate", and this License does not apply to the other self-contained works thus compiled with the Document , on account of their being thus compiled, if they are not themselves derivative works of the Document. If the Cover Text [238] requirement of section 3 is applicable to these copies of the Document, then if the Document is less than one quarter of the entire aggregate, the Document's Cover Texts may be placed on covers that surround only the Document within the aggregate. Otherwise they must appear on covers around the whole aggregate.

8. TRANSLATION

Translation is considered a kind of modification, so you may distribute translations of the Document [238] under the terms of section 4. Replacing Invariant Sections [238] with translations requires special permission from their copyright holders, but you may include translations of some or all Invariant Sections in addition to the original versions of these Invariant Sections. You may include a translation of this License provided that you also include the original English version of this License. In case of a disagreement between the translation and the original English version of this License, the original English version will prevail.

9. TERMINATION

You may not copy, modify, sublicense, or distribute the Document [238] except as expressly provided for under this License. Any other attempt to copy, modify, sublicense or distribute the Document is void, and will automatically terminate your rights under this License. However, parties who have received copies, or rights, from you under this License will not have their licenses terminated so long as such parties remain in full compliance.

10. FUTURE REVISIONS OF THIS LICENSE

The Free Software Foundation [http://www.gnu.org/fsf/fsf.html] may publish new, revised versions of the GNU Free Documentation License from time to time. Such new versions will be similar in spirit to the present version, but may differ in detail to address new problems or concerns. See http://www.gnu.org/copyleft/ [http://www.gnu.org/copyleft].

Each version of the License is given a distinguishing version number. If the Document [238] specifies that a particular numbered version of this License "or any later version" applies to it, you have the option of following the terms and conditions either of that specified version or of any later version that has been published (not as a draft) by the Free Software Foundation. If the Document does not specify a version number of this License, you may choose any version ever published (not as a draft) by the Free Software Foundation.

Addendum

To use this License in a document you have written, include a copy of the License in the document and put the following copyright and license notices just after the title page:

Copyright YEAR YOUR NAME.

Permission is granted to copy, distribute and/or modify this document under the terms of the GNU Free Documentation License, Version 1.1 or any later version published by the Free Software Foundation; with the Invariant Sections [238] being LIST THEIR TITLES, with the Front-Cover Texts [238] being LIST, and with the Back-Cover Texts [238] being LIST. A copy of the license is included in the section entitled "GNU Free Documentation License".

If you have no Invariant Sections [238], write "with no Invariant Sections" instead of saying which ones are invariant. If you have no Front-Cover Texts [238], write "no Front-Cover Texts" instead of "Front-Cover Texts being LIST"; likewise for Back-Cover Texts [238].

If your document contains nontrivial examples of program code, we recommend releasing these examples in parallel under your choice of free software license, such as the GNU General Public License [http://www.gnu.org/copyleft/gpl.html], to permit their use in free software.